Filipino Time

FILIPINO TIME

Affective Worlds and Contracted Labor

ALLAN PUNZALAN ISAAC

Fordham University Press

NEW YORK   2022

Fordham University Press has no responsibility for the persistence or accuracy of URLs for external or third-party Internet websites referred to in this publication and does not guarantee that any content on such websites is, or will remain, accurate or appropriate.

Fordham University Press also publishes its books in a variety of electronic formats. Some content that appears in print may not be available in electronic books.

Visit us online at www.fordhampress.com.

Library of Congress Cataloging-in-Publication Data available online at https://catalog.loc.gov.

Printed in the United States of America

24 23 22   5 4 3 2 1

First edition

To the timely worlds created by
Allyson, Tina, Jillian, Nicole, Liane, and Justin

CONTENTS

Filipino Time

Introduction: Accumulating Time

On August 23, 2010, the Miss Universe Pageant, then a Donald Trump production, aired from Las Vegas, Nevada. In fine Filipino tradition since time immemorial, or at least since when access to a television was possible, many Filipinos around the world gathered to watch their national representative parade in a swimsuit and evening gown. Once a year, a beleaguered global South nation can be as beautiful as and hold its own against any industrialized country, even on the latter's own physically impossible, pristine, patriarchal, and capitalist terms. To be represented in the Miss Universe pageant gives material testament to a nation's market viability, momentarily setting aside the continual monetary devaluations, debt restructuring, crushing poverty, and typhoons and other natural and economic disasters that usually construct and define its tragic image. The double mandate for the national representative is to be both culturally particular and marketably palatable in that difference—to embody fantasy without contradictions, the very work and pleasure of ideology. Miss Philippines that year was Maria Venus Raj, whose planetary and international name preceded by a prayer boded well for the contest but also hinted at her provenance as a daughter of Indian and Filipino workers from Qatar, a child of dispersal and return, violence, and exploitation.

The brightest star in the constellation that night in Las Vegas was Venus, but the YouTube sensation that morning in Manila was four young queer Filipino men who recorded themselves in a reaction video as the much-awaited pageant announced its first cut to the top fifteen semifinalists. The pageant is aired in the early morning in the Philippines. A generic bedroom, pink, perhaps even coral, frames the scene. The four young men sit together on a slightly larger than twin bed in their white pajamas and underwear. The sense of nervous anticipation among the four is palpable. This is a yearly ritual. Literally on the edge of their seats, one young man on the left physically holds himself together. Each figure in the video embodies a bundle of anxieties: pulling at hair, kneeling in a position of prayer, tapping away at the computer, continually touching the face, alternately hyperventilating and not breathing, even nervously picking a nose.

Venus's name is announced. Screams and tears ensue. Amid the bedlam of the bedroom, one man strikes the pose of a beauty pageant winner, containing his unbridled happiness with his hand over his mouth; another is already hard at work spreading the good news across texts and social media. The tears of elation must be cast out into the cloud and out to the virtual universe. The boundless joy is then returned freely and just as quickly from diasporic communities from the Middle East, Australia, the Americas, and Europe and reverberates and builds upon itself to become a perpetual motion machine, energizing itself for itself to exhaustion in the months ahead.

The young men are literally beside themselves over and over again. *Besideness* here signifies the young men's evident emotional excess but also marks the very proliferation of proximities as a mode of celebration: reaching out to one another, reaching out to Venus as adoring fans, reaching out to friends via text, reaching out to strangers and the rest of the world via internet connectivity, reaching out in time to memory making and posterity as the present instantiates its own dispersal to make it more real than real. As Rey Chow observes after Helen Grace: "Capture is what activates reality, what makes reality happen (as in a live performance) in the transitory and vanishing movements of the click, the tap, the pinch, and the fingerswipe."[1] The fan reaction video was tangential to but dependent on the televisual event to record the lived embodiment of the thrill and pride of these young gay Filipino men. The young men's continual activation of media generated this exchange and accumulation of energy to power the event at that moment and weeks into the future. What they captured in the reaction video's wake was not just the event but the affective life of such a national moment, recognizing and reflecting it in the simultaneity and multiplicity of bodily reactions from a bedroom in Southeast Asia to out across Filipino diasporic communities around the world.

Most astonishing in the young gay men's co-performance of joy with the world is that they were not celebrating Miss Philippines winning the pageant (Miss Mexico eventually won) but simply Venus placing in the top fifteen.[2] Hits of their reaction video reached one million views in a day, two million after three days, and almost three million hits six months later. MTV Canada picked it up soon after it went viral, and as one commenter posted:

#68 - Most Discussed (This_ Week))
#13 - Most Discussed (This Week)) - Entertainment
#66 - Most Discussed (This Month)) - Entertainment
#28 - Top Rated (This Week)) - Entertainment
good job!
Lloydie025

These top ratings for the reaction video became as important as Miss Philippines placing in the Miss Universe semifinals. Over six thousand comments accompany the video's YouTube page—conversations mostly in English, Tagalog, Spanish, and Taglish. To be "rated" or to "place" is to appear in the virtual universe, as evidence of recognition that there was not just an empathetic but an enthusiastic audience "out there." The overwhelming number of comments and postings were co-celebrating with the four young men in the release and exchange of untrammeled joy throughout pockets of Filipino migrant communities in Dubai, Hong Kong, Sydney, and many other places.

Many Philippine households are supported by family members working abroad. Cash sent home by overseas Filipinos through banks hit a record $26.9 billion in 2016, up 5 percent from 2015.[3] Personal remittances from the 10 percent of the population that lives abroad account for almost 10 percent of the national GDP.[4] Remittances drive domestic consumption and keep the economy of the Philippine archipelago afloat. Every day, six thousand Filipinos processed by POEA leave the Philippines to work as contract workers abroad.[5] From domestic training and governmental bureaucracies to foreign financial and commercial outreach targeted to potential emigrants, the government and oligarchic elite of labor-exporting countries optimize the conditions by which exporting labor becomes the national comparative advantage to compete in the global marketplace. Initiated by the US-backed Marcos regime in 1974, the out-migration of skilled workers was a way to quell domestic unrest and unemployment as well as a response to debt restructuring. Subsequent administrations have taken up what was then a temporary solution to consolidate the brokerage state.

Besideness is also the nation's identification with Maria Venus Raj, herself a product of temporary migrant laborers. Daughter of a single mother, a tenant farmer, her Cinderella story is the stuff of Filipino *teleseryes*, or soap operas. But her road to the Philippine crown was as muddy as the rice field on which she claimed to practice her winning walk. Venus was *not* a *native* daughter. Venus was born in Doha, Qatar—a product of a possibly violent encounter between her mother, a domestic helper working in Qatar from 1986 to 1988, and an Indian national, reportedly an architect named Vincent Raj. Venus's family was evasive about the identity of the father; Venus claimed all photos of him were lost in a fire in her hometown in the southern Luzon region. A month after giving birth to Venus, the mother returned to her rural village, San Vicente, Camarines Sur. The youngest of five children, Venus and her family continued as tenant farmers and moved around the area when they were unable to make payments. She later secured a scholarship to study at the local college, where she graduated cum laude with a degree in journalism. At five feet, nine inches, taller than the average Filipina, she started entering local beauty pageants at age seventeen. Stories circulated about how she used her winnings at local pageants to buy land and build her mother a house.

Venus finally won the coveted title of Miss Philippines Universe in 2010 at the age of twenty-one, but twenty-three days later she was dethroned when it was discovered that her birth certificate gave false information about her origins. The birth certificate stated that she had been born in her rural town and that her father was also Filipino. But during the pageant preinterview she admitted to pageant officials that she had been born in Qatar, out of wedlock, to a foreign father. Her birth certificate, it was later revealed, had been filed by an aunt three years after her birth. Less than a month after her victory, pageant officials asked her to resign her title or be dethroned. She was also asked not to explain why she had resigned lest vicious gossip come out about her illegitimate birth. Venus chose to be dethroned rather than resign and went to lawyers and the press. Her rural hometown supporters, mentors, and scholarship supporters, as well as politicians and public figures, came together in her defense. A public outcry ensued. The hometown of San Vicente welcomed her back with great fanfare, fifty children from different neighborhoods presenting her with flowers as an expression of love for their daughter and sister.

Diasporic netizenship brought Venus Raj a second triumph. Bloggers, writers, websites, and a signature campaign on Facebook started by fans in her rural province but gathering force around the globe: Here was a poor rural girl being belittled and oppressed by the Manila-centric middle classes, who cared nothing about beauty and hard work but only sought hypocritical respectability. The Miss Universe–Binibining Pilipinas franchise issued a statement that the reason for her dethronement was that her documents were falsified. Here was a young woman who used her beauty and talent to defy the odds and make it out of poverty to conquer the world—so the lore goes. Venus Raj beat the odds not just regarding poverty but also regarding the sheer physical impossibility of being 5'9", 110 lbs, in a nation, if not a universe, where such anatomical measurements are well-nigh impossible. The masses had spoken, and they wanted her as their queen. On May 21, after eleven days, the Miss Universe franchise relented, declaring that if Venus Raj could secure a Philippine passport showing her citizenship, she would be reinstated as Miss Philippines. A small rural region emerged victorious in redefining what nationalism meant against the capital region. Maria Venus Raj represented more than the respectable citizenship the franchise purportedly desired. The small town and the internet activism calling upon a Filipino global audience were able to shift the terms and terrain of national belonging along class lines. Hers became a story of outsiders, migrants, the poor, those born outside marriage calling out the elite's moral hypocrisy to claim a place in national representation. Briefly she made the outlines of that dispersed national body wider and legible, as a cause of the downtrodden. She unapologetically embodied not only the genetic and peripatetic circuit of the labor diaspora but also its pain, violence, and travails, discriminated against in terms of class, national belonging, and moral bearings.

As internet sensations watching this drama unfold triumphantly on the global stage, the young men, *bakla*, boisterous, and equally as unapologetic as Venus, are precisely that which cannot enter that pageant franchise's visual field for capital consumption and profit. The beauty queen must be the symbol of a national body rendered intelligible, colonially disciplined, and contained for international consumption. The compelling nature of the video is the recognition of what could not be properly exhibited—underwear, nervous tics, unrestrained joy.[6] Venus Raj embodied others' fantasies, whereas the young men enact the excesses of these fantasies. It is this excess that viewers sought to reflect and celebrate in return through comments, hits, and repeated plays. The viewer took pleasure precisely because these bodies do not respect the conventions of masculinity or consumer femininity, especially in the moment of elation— leaping on beds, falling on the floor, the cries of "Thank you, Lord," making signs of the cross, uncontrolled weeping, hyperventilating. The joy reaches outside the pink bedroom immediately, dispersed through phone calls, texts, Twitter, Facebook, and other social media.

Symbiotic projects such as Venus and the fan reaction video are not just about aspiration but are modes of affective exchange that have lives beyond and beside capital productions: lives in likes, shares, comments, and reposts.[7] If the hand flailing, the exuberance, the tears, and the joy enact exponentially what Venus cannot manifest as the commodified Miss Universe, the video reached out to a virtual universe. Multiply wired even as they watched the pageant, the four young men sought to gather their expanded imagined community and their communities of imagination. The young men framed and recorded themselves, edited and made the video public to gather fans but also to share that moment of jubilation across the world over and over. Celebrating the placing of Venus, a child of poverty and labor dispersal, insists on having that "place" register. It is to cause a sensation, "for you to feel them feeling you," as Moten and Harney define hapticality. To stake a "place," as Venus had, and be rated on the internet platform, as had the fan video, was to achieve legibility in disarticulation, in both the senses of dispersal and euphoria. The fan video's enthusiastic dispersal reverberates with affective accretion and exchange along the platforms of global capital.

Filipino Time examines how immaterial labor, service work that does not produce physical commodities, performed by Filipinos in the Philippines and around the world, while producing bodily and affective disciplines and dislocations, also generates vital affects, other chronicities, multiple networks, and other worlds. Life-making capacities lie within the capitalist world of disruptions and trade of bodies and time. Because intersubjective interaction and creative capacities are part of care labor, the feeling of time is indeterminate and multivalent. Subjects make worlds out of one colonized by capital time. Alongside but also beyond capitalist intention and national territories, Venus and the viral fan video proffer other relations to and senses of time to make palpable a global present and presence. Aligned with each other at points, both stories signal the creative capacities of life making and social networking. Projected from on stage and the televisual to YouTube and the smartphone, the elements of communality—a precarious and often temporary gathering of the imagination—take shape. The present in its proliferative visibility on digital platforms in the contemporary era acquires multiple lives that rub up against multiple audiences at once. Foucault announced in his 1967 lecture "Of Other Spaces": "We are in the epoch of simultaneity; we are in the epoch of juxtaposition, the epoch of the near and far, of the side by side, of the dispersed."[8] Foucault here speaks of time and space at once to signal how networks make simultaneity and juxtapositions possible even in dispersal, thus widening the scope of the socialities and trans-subjectivities we can imagine. Within the layers of telecommunications, social media, and other forms of movement, these reconfigurations produce various forms of ephemeral proximity and intimacy across multiple temporalities that illuminate new gatherings and subjectivities not otherwise recognizable or legible. Each instance of contact calls on another type of audience to experience the play with time. Being side by side on multiple platforms underscores how time, space, and the disruptions of these are experienced bodily and together.

Digital connectivity, as one mode of sociality, made it possible for both Venus and the fan video to exist side by side, to be beside each other—manifestations of the same doubled gaze—as other scenes of meaning making. The young men made evident their global present. Considering the power of digital capture, Rey Chow suggests, "Conceptualizing the present as a collective but diffused assemblage of enunciation, one that may be snatched in bits at a time and then plugged into a mutating plenitude of virtualities."[9] These "bits" take on lives of their own. This plenitude recalls what Édouard Glissant has described as "wild forms of accumulation, the excessiveness of an unexpected and unstoppable flow." Indeed, the young men's video displayed and generated excess but also elicited admiration and joy from across the globe in return. This wild accumulation of the imagination across media platforms enabled various modes of experiencing elation and the world.[10] What emerged in this exchange was the world's imaginability *with others*. The moment's diffusion to multiple network platforms created new proximities and suggests the vital force in the asynchrony of ideological image and lived practices and excesses. Life-making socialities are unexpectedly catalyzed by capital relations.

There are other ways to feel time.[11] As literature and other cultural expressions have allowed us to experience, time is not simply about before and after, a sequential unfolding; it can be extended, arrested, and snapped. The exuberance and play that the young men generated and shared insist that there are other deployments and trajectories for bodies beyond the productive demands of nationalism and capitalism. These deployments and trajectories, rather than simply militarized metaphors, are not necessarily against but alongside the demands of global capital, patriarchy, and nationalism. Perhaps that instant in the slippery yet full global present contains the opening to these other places and times. That instant allows other ways to feel time. This queer sensibility insists that, in Jose Muñoz's words, "the present is not enough."[12] And perhaps the making-present also contains a multitude of communal possibilities that engage with what Muñoz terms as "collective temporal distortion."[13]

Affective Labor and Affect

Away from Venus's runway and the young men's pink bedroom, under the relentless rumble of the 7 train in Woodside, Queens, are thousands of Filipinos not as visible to a global audience but just as connected to a global network every single day. In April 2016, the *New Yorker* published Rachel Aviv's "The Cost of Caring: The Lives of Immigrant Women Who Tend to the Needs of Others," about one of the many Filipina migrant workers who keep households and global economies running.[14]

> More than thirteen thousand Filipinos live in the blocks surrounding Roosevelt Avenue, under the tracks of the No. 7 subway line, which takes them to Times Square. The avenue has evolved to meet the needs of female migrants: there's a shop specializing in uniforms for nannies, housekeepers, and home health aides, and several freight and remittance centers, where workers send their earnings and gifts to their families.

Subway and commuter lines transport Filipinas and other women of color to other homes, where they work as caregivers and domestics; freight and remittance centers keep money and goods circulating; Skype and other digital platforms keep love flowing. Aviv offers a moving portrait of middle-aged Emma, from Bukidnon, Philippines, the mother of nine daughters. Once an ambitious young woman, an avid reader of novels, Emma and her husband simply could not earn enough from her government post as a nutritionist and his seasonal earnings from his family farm to provide for the family. Following her sister, a former teacher, and many other women in her town, she migrated to New York, finding a job as a caregiver for children and older adults in private homes. The article covers the struggles with US immigration agencies as a working person, Emma's love for the children she cares for, and the difficulties of remote mothering, all issues that Rhacel Parreñas, Valerie Francisco, and other scholars of domestic migration have astutely explored.

Amid the background of loneliness away from her children and the cycle of poverty that would drive her townmates and some of their daughters to the same fate, the last third of Aviv's article focuses on a special bond that develops between Emma and Ivy, a younger caregiver. They develop an intimate relationship, referring to each other as adoptive mother and daughter. The writer seems to suggest more than a mother-daughter bond in this relationship, but these familial terms would be the only acceptable ones for Emma, who has just gotten a divorce (not recognized in the Philippines) from her husband, and Ivy, who remains faithfully married to a man back in the Philippines. The author describes the two women sharing a twin bed; Emma's niece sleeps on the top bunk. The relationship develops: Ivy quits her job in Long Island and gets another in the city so she can move in with Emma in Queens. Their bond becomes the primary one, over those in the Philippines and those with the children at work: "At night, if Ivy went to bed before talking to Emma, she kept her cell phone by her pillow and woke up periodically to check for messages. 'If I don't talk to her one day, I'm not comfortable,' Ivy told me. 'I feel like there is something missing.'"[15] While being connected to others is part of the job's skill set, the same bonding mechanism is also a way for Emma and Ivy to feel human and alive for and with each other, either on digital platforms or on platform beds.

What sleeps and breathes alongside labor-time in care labor?

Affect names connections, feelings, moving bodies, bodies being moved, and bodies going outside their putative boundaries. Thus, it speaks to the global migration of labor and the new socialities generated by these movements. Much of the shared love returned to the young men through the fan video came from pockets of Filipino communities in other parts of Asia, Europe, the Middle East, and the United States, and each became visible to the others. The late-twentieth- and twenty-first-century shift to flexible labor has forced migration scholars, as the cultural critic Theodore Gonzalves describes in the context of Filipino performance, to focus on "new kinds of communities being built, contextualized, and imagined in locales that reflect rooting and routing throughout the world."[16] Scholars of Filipino studies have focused on the conditions that make the in-between within and across nation-states possible. To think through relations "in between" suggests multiple possibilities and potential mutual transformations and gatherings. As I explore in Chapter 2 in short stories about Filipinos across time and countries, the in-between is composed of chronic cumulations and turns—intensity, direction, and diffusion. Multiple intimacies and histories rub up against one another and enable temporary collectivities and affinities in the time-space compression of globalization. The focus on affect highlights the trans-subjective experience that bodies, objects, and sociohistorical conditions make possible. While affect articulates the capacity and possibility of bodies, sometimes intentional but often not, it also traces noncorporeal forces like ambience, feel, and atmosphere. Bodily senses and sense making become an interface for ways to be in the world to mark and take up durations and spaces.

Much migrant Filipino labor is paid to make time for others. As speculative capital, Filipino caregivers, domestics, nurses, teachers, and other service workers around the world have been ensconced in these care in-dustries economies for decades. "Affective labor," Michael Hardt asserts, "has assumed a dominant position with respect to other forms of labor in the global capitalist economy."[17] Social reproduction is quantified, val-uated, and exchanged on a global scale. For the host country, Filipinos arrive in the form of commodified labor, wherein lifetimes and acquired knowledge are translated into usable labor. The Philippines as a broker-age state not only trains workers for the global marketplace but also disciplines these temporary workers to remain linked financially and emotionally back to the Philippines.[18] For the Philippines, many Filipi-nos "return" in the form of remittances. Remittances translate social cap-ital, futurity, and distance into a representation of value. The abstract expression of value—money—always supplements bodily arrivals and returns. In this exchange, the Filipino body is asynchronous, never quite arriving or returning. She is always a custodial subject—surveilled, managed, administered, extracted. This is the story globalization makes apparent.

However, care labor involves textural aspects of living felt in touch, sight, smell, and sound across different platforms. Like Emma and Ivy's relationship, this so-called labor of love is as vast as the subjects them-selves. Care labor makes visible how interpellation into capital involves multiple parts of human cognitive ability. Sara Ahmed has provided an elegant exposition on the relationship between directionality and perfor-mativity.[19] The bodily twists that interpellation demands define phe-nomenologically what is proximate, visible, and thinkable for the subject. This impetus to "hear oneself as the subject of address" and the direction of the turn to the discourse are performed with varying degrees of inten-sity according not only to what is prohibited, permitted, and required but also to what the subject desires in terms of survival and pleasure.[20] Care work is not repetitive, mechanical, skilled labor housed in the fac-tory. Other and more human capacities, especially the capacity to dream and improvise, are called upon to be used and developed to do care work effectively.

To be alongside, to be with another, opens up a whole host of possible engagements and visions because it is relational and juxtapositional. Eve Sedgwick in *Touching Feeling* signals how proximity itself is generative of action and feeling because "it comprises a wide range of desiring, identi-fying, representing, repelling, paralleling, differentiating, rivalling, lean-ing, twisting, mimicking, withdrawing, attracting, aggressing, warping, and other relations."[21] I note that each of Sedgwick's gerunds—desiring, rivaling, twisting, aggressing—forges not only a relational affect but also *a temporality*. These relations lay open a range that we can imagine against, alongside, and outside of the so-called march of time. They achieve semblance, distinction, or distortion depending on how the parties imagine their relationship to and in time—together. She continues:

> What is crucial to queer relationality is not only the act of comparison, but a critical examination of the space "in between," which is not a space separating discrete categories, bodies, or languages, but binds, transforms, and translates them quite queerly. How might an emphasis on relationality demonstrate, in new ways, the multiplicity of inflections and intersections between gender, sexuality, race, ethnicity, national and religious affiliation, and disability? Finally, what are some of the political stakes of a relational analysis, when we consider, for example, relations of language and violence and other power relations? To what extent can the relational, the trans, the liminal, the mediating space "in between" operate as a potential site of rupture, of epistemological or social transformation?[22]

In examining the potential ruptures in binding, translation, and transformation, I also scrutinize the social conditions of the mediating space and the work necessary to make even conflictive relationships happen. Tense proximities and chosen kinships generate ethical and temporal formations. Being in apposition, rather than simply crossing or intersecting, is not static but intimates a duration and prolonged negotiation and also opens the variety and degrees of proximity, anywhere from the contingent to the discontiguous, from the causal to the (non)coincidental.

Affect thus limns the subtle and not-so-subtle shifts in mood and modes that frame relationships and ways of being in the world. Care labor creates relationships and manipulates affect.[23] Affect has intensity and direction, that is, vectors. The direction may be multiple and, oftentimes, diffuse. This affective redirection meets the contractual obligation of conjuring proximity with another human being but also carves another chronicity and space for the worker within the contracted work time. These granular shifts nuance how we understand subjects interpellated by multiple locations and normative identities in terms of nation, gender, sexuality, race, and class. Indeed, affect is the cumulation of effects influencing and generating emotions, feelings, and conditions around work and migration that issue from the social and political as well as from the local and granular. Yet subjects remain irreducible to these calcified categories.

The inherent creativity that is part of contemporary care labor generates unquantifiable vital forms in everyday work and living.[24] Rather than the impoverishment of the senses and desensitization of the worker to mental passivity, sensitivity and the capacity to anticipate desire is cultivated and valued. In creating proximity, one orients the body to another and shares life and time trans-subjectively. Care and service workers, as I will explore in the call center industry and among caregivers in Israel, and their ways of taking up various spaces make evident the permeability across bodies and cultures.[25] In terms of gendered labor, the protocols of care are directed by the employer, the institution, and the state to define the shape of the relational landscape.[26] How one performs tasks of care and relationship to others is defined by local criteria. That is, the practice and limits of care are not universal but rather are dictated by the values and norms of local culture and state regulation and therefore require bodily and cultural translation on the part of the care-agent. Bodily and cultural translation and improvisation involve creative capacities. While work time has been purchased and contracted for the activity to take place, the qualitative texture of the time, its chronicity, shared with others is in the realm of action, creativity, and meaning making of the subject.

Affective Labor and Other Senses of Time

In contrast to mechanistic, Fordist production, producing intimacies and ways of being-with-others generates its own ethical and chronic configurations that condition proximity. Emma and Ivy in Queens, New York, turn to each other and their families back in the Philippines as responses to work life. They turn to various affective worlds at once. Care labor, the act of conjuring proximity and propinquity, is multidimensional, thus giving an infinite variety of textures to the feeling of time with another. Though the production of emotional bonds is quantified, parsed, waged, and extracted in the global labor market, its qualitative complexity cannot be wholly captured and exhausted. I draw attention here to affective worlds that could provide insight into other human capacities wielded within state and economic constraints.

In contracting labor, a capitalist assumes that the laborer enters into a contract to sell her labor time. Marx's concept of labor-time translates virtually all human activity and signification into capital value. Marx also conceptualizes "abstract labor" to describe how capital homogenizes human activity and artistry toward the creation of commodities for circulation and profit. The contract defines limited forms of relations out of all possible ones and therefore devalues other forms of labor that might also be socially necessary. Labor-time is a concept that has duration, in which something is transformed (produced) to effect the fulfillment of the contract. Therefore, the worker contracts her time and, more particularly, her body *in time*. The work contract, I would then add, may also be thought to contract (to limit) the meaning of the output and creative possibilities of the laboring body in time, since the interest of the contractor sets the rules of what and how interaction and sociality is to be produced and made meaningful. Therefore a whole set of possibilities and meanings are made valueless, or at least illegible, when rules bracket off nonproductive meanings to be assigned to a set of actions.[27] Outside this limited understanding of action and meanings are submerged exchanges and dynamic, uneven movements that exceed the logic of capital capture and legibility.

Feminist scholars, scholars of the Asian diasporas, and post-Marxists have challenged Marx's nineteenth-century definition of labor-time. Labor-time in his labor theory of value is the abstracted duration of human labor necessary to create value for a commodity. Early on in her feminist scholarship, Arlie Hochschild problematizes the valuation and measure of feminized labor that requires customers in certain affective states.[28] Given the paradoxical character of care labor, the work of social reproduction might be devalued, yet its value is continually negotiated and exchanged in the world market, harnessing and trading the work and time of women, people of color, and immigrants. Sarita See in *Filipino Primitive* revisits primitive accumulation to reveal how capital is not inevitable but rather an open system that must renew itself continually by acts of devaluation and dispossession.[29] Massimiliano Tomba, in his work *Marx's Temporalities*, asserts that there are always worker countertimes (strikes, work delays, in his examples), as well as nonmodern temporalities (different modes of exchange), continually at play with and against one another. The state forges, he argues, a "violent synchronization of different historical temporalities."[30] With Marx's concept model, some progressive critiques of capital continue to focus on and replicate the centrality of capital's narrative of time, production, and its effects. For example, Kathi Weeks diagnosed correctly early on that nonalienation from work cannot be the hallmark of progressive labor politics.[31] While necessary, the call for better working conditions and worker participation in production also serves to make capital machinery more efficient. The idea of making work less alienated and alienating hits its limit as human resources and management discourse tamps down and obscures the violence that Tomba points to as a primary state function.

Iyko Day's *Alien Labor* locates the initial capitalist violence in the very abstraction of labor into money wages: "Capital maximizes profit by controlling time: socially necessary labor time."[32] Time, like bodies, is racialized and assigned differential value before and at the abstraction of labor-time. This nuance underscores how embedded in the "socially necessary" is the racial distribution of meaning assigned to types of labor and time. Performed by women and migrants from economically disadvantaged parts of the world, the devaluation of labor begins with the devaluation of gendered and racialized geographic locations and its inhabitants. This emphasis on devaluation underscores seemingly nonproductive relations that go into the creation of value.

Care labor as part of migratory and human resource trade blurs the line between productive and reproductive labor, between working and living.[33] Labor-time and other times do not necessarily cleave. Rather, multiple life-times and vital exchanges are copresent within it. Drawing from Paulo Virno, the critical theorist Neferti Tadiar forces us to see "production time" without the strict separation between labor and nonlabor time, or, as she describes, remunerated and nonremunerated time.[34] Exchange of labor-time into the money form is only one way of abstracting value. Human activity bears "plural qualities, conditions, and effects," Tadiar reminds us.[35] Time, therefore, is not only money as abstract value but encompasses capacities and the qualitative formation of other values and exchanges; these force us to reconsider what comprises the "socially necessary" in labor time.

Focusing on value, however, makes invisible the subject herself, who must continue to thrive under exploitative conditions. What might be more worthwhile beyond alienation and disalienation is to formulate a different relation between life and work. Franco Berardi refers to post-Fordist modes of production as semiocapitalism, which "takes the mind, language and creativity as its primary tools for the production of value."[36] It is not only the body of the worker but her creativity, skill, knowledge, and movement in contracted time that go into creating a product or service. Affective labor involves a wide range of human capacities, making it difficult to determine what global capital captures and what it cannot. Creative labor and exchanges are not entirely translated into the abstract expression of money quantification. Uncaptured human capacity of meaning making opens up other ways to feel the direction and intensities of time. I would suggest other ways to imagine the relationship between living and work, embedded and co-opted unevenly as part of the psychic and material life of care labor.

Affective Labor and Communality

Care labor is trans-subjective. It traffics in human emotions and vital expressions. As Emma and Ivy create affective connections with their charges and each other, affective labor, as Hardt and Negri have observed, holds the promise of communicative and interactive cooperation that is inherent in the work itself.[37] Here lies the force of interactive workplaces populated by women and feminized labor:

> What affective labor produces are social networks, forms of community, biopower. Here one might recognize once again that the instrumental action of economic production has been united with the communicative action of human relations; in this case, however communication has not been impoverished, but production has been enriched to the level of complexity of human interaction.[38]

The dominance of service work introduces and develops cooperation networks among people as part of what is to be harnessed by capital. These intermittent relations are vital given their critical place in capitalist production, and these intimacies underscore how outsourced activity by feminized labor from the global South serves oftentimes as the only living, human aspect of the lightning speed of capitalist consumption of goods, technology, and services.

Hospitals, private homes, and care homes are sites of labor by women, migrants, and other feminized labor. As other-sites of society, these "heterotopias," as Foucault has described, "are most often linked to slices in time—which is to say they open onto what might be termed, for the sake of symmetry, heterochronicities."[39] These slices in time index other ways to sense time in these care work spaces, ways often dictated by industry forces. In the same essay, Foucault also signals the existence of other slices of time aside from heterotopias: "Opposite these heterotopias that are linked to the accumulation of time, there are those that are linked to time in its most fleeting, transitory, precarious aspect, to time in the mode of the festival."[40] I am less interested in the carnivalesque or the festival and more in how the everyday is textured so that the "fleeting, transitory, precarious aspect" of time has places of habitability and bearability for migrant labor in these spaces.

As demonstrated by the wild accumulation of imagination by Venus and the fan video, there exist life exchanges among dispersed, migrant communities that insist upon a complex of interconnected subjects that generate moments of pleasure and creative connections. The dispersal and deployment of immaterial labor is a necessary process to achieve time-space compression, but viewed from labor's vantage point, time and space become refracted and disjointed concepts that reorganize subjects' bodies and relations. These fractured conditions bring to the fore more imaginative ways to create and manipulate human relationships. Even in these contracted spaces, "life is porous, shareable across persons, trans-missible across distances of space and time, renewable, and multipliable," as Tadiar has described.[41] As feminists and critical race studies scholars have shown, capital comes in many self-contradictory forms. Similarly, vitality too comes in multiple qualitative forms. Grace Hong rightfully observes how the culture of neoliberalism has disciplined our "sense of sociality and futurity" as forms of economic value: "We can also think of neoliberalism as characterized by the proliferation of various forms of value within the economic."[42] The "sense of sociality and futurity" is an organizing principle and material network of conditions that makes some-thing thinkable and imaginable. What of things not yet translatable or that indeed must remain dormant and emergent to become meaningful and have effect? These circulate differently. Echoing feminist work on the care industries, Hardt signals how "affective labour produces social net-works, forms of community, biopower."[43] Operating on the somatic as well as communal level, care work is the creative labor necessary to connect with people, to establish relationships, and to project futures for others and ourselves that guide the everyday. Therefore, the challenge is to glean the life and meaning making that capital fails to assimilate as part of pro-ductive labor-time.

Stories like that of Emma and Ivy give account of other modes of af-fective exchange (rather than production), which create proximities that register alternative, lived proximities, chronicities, and meanings for their lives. These socialities are not necessarily anticapitalist, and for migrant workers this form of communal reciprocity and life making cannot pre-sume community. I do not use the word "community" so readily and in-stead use "communality" to indicate ways of interaction or a coming together that might be conditional, temporary, and contingent. Alterna-tive affective exchanges issue from spaces steeped in global capital but are never quite fully captured within capital's quantifying grasp. Indeed, these spaces are the excluded spaces created by global capital itself. In the subsequent chapters, I highlight details of cultural expressions, practices, and narratives that might be deemed unimportant and perhaps discon-tiguous with imperialist productions. In reading these cultural produc-tions, I look for traces of these other concurrent chronicities, ways of sensing and making sense of time alongside capital's dominant narrative.[44] From the hostile but habitable textures of labor-time, migratory subjects live and weave narratives of place and belonging, produce new modes of connections and ways to feel time with others. Here we get a glimpse of the surplus value of life; that is, the qualitative feel and meaning of time, quite distinct from its quantification measured by time served, given, and produced as and for work. Vital chronicities represent such unaccounted surplus that circulates, forms, and takes various shapes among people.

Expressive cultures explore animating lifeworlds in these other intimacies despite and because of temporary contracts, wars, disputed borders, and dislocation. I focus on the qualitative life- and meaning-making capacities of Filipina, queer subjects, and producers of the cultural works I examine. I argue that various types of proximities texture temporalities issuing from contractual and familial obligations and beyond, that other ways to "make time" in these socialities and exchanges are generated alongside labor-time beyond sanctioned care, and that expressive culture uncovers these unintended or occluded exchanges and relationships issuing from these forced proximities to highlight different meanings assigned to migrant bodies beyond either heroic labor or national threat but also a source and way to tell stories. As Gayatri Gopinath has argued, "It is in the realm of the aesthetic that we can excavate these submerged, comingled histories and become attuned to their continuing resonance in the present as they echo across both bodies and landscapes."[45] Inscribed in cultural expressions about care labor, in which millions of Filipino migrants are ensconced—care and domestic work, teaching, call centers— these forms of living show how selves go out of bounds beyond the economic contract to transform even momentarily self, others, time, and their surroundings.

As with Venus and the fan video and Emma and Ivy, these nonnormative forms of generating vitality offer alternative ways of making sense—both meaning and feeling—of dislocation. They excavate the social cumulations that are obscured or lost in translation to "socially necessary" labor-time in the traditional Marxist understanding of creating "value." Cultural expressions capture ephemera; reveal multiple affects and chronicities, the feel of durations experienced by the subject; and offer glimpses into emergent relations and social formations. These vital expressions potentially reveal and revel in the other ways diasporics create human value and meaning beyond market logics and resistance. Thus my focus frames performative moments of waiting, refusal, self-enjoyment, excess, and even death conditioned by capital quantification as spaces and times that also encompass qualitative elements of human interaction captured by artists. These various disruptions, deployments, and senses of time rub up alongside, even make way for, an in-between historical chronicity for the lived experience of migratory life.

As is well documented among transnational and migration scholars, contemporary migration is inextricably tied to globalization and nation-state technologies of assimilation and exclusion.[46] Global economies stage bodily proximities, from teachers in Baltimore, Maryland, to caregivers in Tel Aviv, and subjectivities are shaped by the political economy at home and abroad—yet migrants and workers disrupt national spaces and times, too. While sending and receiving nation-states manage and enforce flow and new proximities, given the nature of care work, subjects too exert force and shape how events, spaces, and other people relate to one another. The performative, visual, and cultural expressions described in this book capture how bodies and time are disjoined or conjoined in novel ways to inhabit these worlds. Deploying interdisciplinary methodology from close readings to ethnography, each chapter examines cultural works set in the Philippines, the United States, and the Middle East to show how subjects imagine and sense themselves in simultaneity and in juxtaposition to others. Each takes a different genre and analyzes the cultural discourse surrounding the care industry and the various chronicities imagined around the work to limn the contours of various communalities under contracted time.

Chapter Synopses

Filipino Time claims that affective communal worlds are rendered palpable through these creative productions and phenomena that generate, disrupt, and expand the experience of time. The book explores how these modes of making time and proximities are rearticulated in a capacious archive of storytelling about the Filipino labor diaspora in fiction, a musical, an ethnography, and a documentary film. The chapters that follow look at cultural works that explore affective regimes of daily life: emotional deferral, pivots, disruptions, temporal leaps, living deaths. Creative moments, opportune ones, as I explore in Chapter 2, emerge from and even work alongside dominant ways of being in the world but might feel differently—even feel multiply and metaphysically—whether in fantasies about death in a musical (Chapter 4) or while keeping work time and corporate futures at bay in a call center (Chapter 3).

The Filipino vernacular concept *dating* captures a person's composure, arrival, and impact on a place and on the others around them. Thus someone's arrival also becomes a moment of other possibilities. Using

Ramona Diaz's documentary *The Learning* (2011), Chapter 1 explores the migrant subject's capacity to capture these occasional moments of temporal plenitude within contractual time. *The Learning* tells the story of Filipina schoolteachers from across the Philippine archipelago who were recruited to Baltimore's struggling and de facto racially segregated public schools. Much of the film's narrative is focused on the maintenance of kinship across great distances, employing back-and-forth splices; the film also spends much time on the subjects' performative gestures, which redirect narratives away from well-worn tropes of duty, resistance and self-sacrifice. *Dating* indexes the body's capacity to configure space, arrivals, returns, and atmosphere to stage other worlds. Thus, instead of focusing on the teachers' return narratives as the primary focal point of redirection, I read the passing but self-staging performative moments in the film through Diaz's cutting and splicing to shed light on the ways subjects control time and wrest the story away from an overarching national or labor narrative.

Dating, as composure and arrival, conceptualizes time not simply as a passing duration but also as timing. In classical rhetoric, *kairos*, or timeliness, is that intangible eventuality not wholly about individual intent but the deployment of social conditions to configure possibilities for the moment. Chapter 2 considers *kairos*, that is, timing or timeliness, as a qualitative experience of time in three short stories about Filipinos in different types of service work: Mia Alvar's "The Miracle Worker," in her short story collection *In the Country: Stories* (2015), about exiles, emigrants, and wanderers in Bahrain, the United States, and the Philippines; Michelle Cruz Skinner's "In the Company of Strangers," the title short story triptych in the eponymous collection about domestic workers in Italy; and Nicholas Go's flash fiction "The Blind Oracle of Mactan," about a long-lived but youthful masseur who can foretell the future. In these narratives of economy, I highlight how the authors nuance the moment of insight to draw attention to in-between times—speculation, meantimes, and conjoined futurity. These timely frictions in fiction bring to light vital exchanges and value making that generate possibilities for world making and communing otherwise.

Chapter 3 explores how ethnography might serve as a chronography, a thick and textured accounting of time. Through discourse analysis and ethnography, the offshore identity of call center agents emerges from partial and temporal, rather than spatial, migration into the global simultaneity of times as well as into global and national contestation over the worker's representation. Nationalism fuses with capitalist rhetoric to produce fantasies of development for the middle- and lower-middle-class denizens of Manila and Cebu. However, for the worker, these global futures are simply the creation of more disruptive times and imagined endings. While extending national space, the offshore generated by the simultaneity of times bridged by twenty-first-century technology is non-identical with either national or global time. This chronography captures the vernacular feel and friction not only of place and time but also of timely durations in the offshore, from the three-hundred-second (five-minute) call it generates to the various futurities it proffers.

Chapter 4 takes up affective redirections explored by a musical staged in Manila about queer Filipino caregivers in Israel. This chapter is informed by interviews with the director and writer of the musical *Care Divas*, based in Manila, as well as with Filipino caregivers in Israel. The musical brings global migration and the regional politics of the Palestinian-Israeli conflict into queer spaces, times, and communities. While death is always a possibility in war and within contract labor's precarious condition in a war zone, the plot's "refusal to wallow," as per the director, in the face of tragedies generates the emergence of other ways to form communalities, even life, amid annihilation. The musical plays with stopping, extending, disembodying, retelling, and making impossible the life and time(s) of the protagonists. My focus on death and its various stagings examines how the work avoids falling into the pitfalls of the hero/victim binary and other narratives that secure nationalist fantasies. Indeed, relationships in the plot run awry of state-sanctioned relationships and show how family and nation as precarious fictions give way to temporary collectivities that find life in the musical's virtual time and place.

I end with a Coda, which looks at a mediated mourning practice in the Philippines, *e-burol*, that is, live-streamed funeral vigils, a common, now decade-old technological practice made necessary by Filipino diasporic life, to explore various embodied conceptions of sociality and relationality when time and space do not coincide but are juxtaposed through a mediated interface. Since the medium affords entry and exit into various modes of time—ritual time, everyday time, and end times, *e-burol* makes manifest various ways of being with others. I highlight two Tagalog concept-words that map other ways to generate ecologies of communality. *Pakiramdam* (literally, to make oneself felt, or to feel a presence) is affective engagement without immediate proximity at all; *kapiling*, with the collectivizing *ka-* prefix, is to be in someone's proximity or vicinity, but the connotation does not necessarily include or demand any interaction between the two parties.

Each of the chapters traces moments of communing, transition, and becoming of subjects under global capital conditions. The human touch of care labor, in time, space, and with others, is extracted and often disappears into and acts as extensions of global North capacities, but the queer men and women, and migrants conjuring and generating this human touch populate, live, and feel in the constrained spaces of this very erasure. They all share these conditions of touch and erasure at once. Fred Moten redefines the haptic in the undercommons in terms of affect and recognition:

> Hapticality, the touch of the undercommons, the interiority of the sentiment, the feel that what is to come is here. Hapticality, the capacity to feel through others, for others to feel through you, for you to feel them feeling you, this feel of the shipped is not regulated, at least not successfully by a state, a religion, a people, an empire, a piece of land, a totem.[47]

Moten and Harney's poetic description gets at the heart of this project, in which timely redirections, cumulated intensity, and turns mark joy, spirit, and being with others in communal but temporary worlds. These creative acts redistribute the power of touch to other spaces and times that are not necessarily part of capital productivity but forms of life that emerge from it. While human touch is produced, commodified, and exported, then erased and disposed as needed, its vitality in creating human relationships is deployed for both capital and multiple noncapital ends often simultaneously. The mediating tool, whether film, musical, stories, or song, that these subjects deploy renders visible creative and life-making capacities apposite and alongside capital production.

Communality is the precarious, oftentimes fleeting gathering of the imagination, wherein human beings reach out to touch others. Unregulated hapticality, to return to Moten and Stefano's formulation of "the touch of the undercommons," is the interiority of the sentiment, the feel that what is to come is here. Venus, the fan reaction video, and Emma's bedside texts to Ivy are durational moments that transform and announce that "what is to come is here."[48] With its multiple directions and intensities, the ecology of affective labor generates many ways to sense time to reveal how the body can bear the slow cumulation of timely permutations that can suddenly open us to other worlds—together.

1 /   "I've Never Been to Me":
Redirecting Arrivals and Returns

> In capitalist society, free time is produced for one class by the
> conversion of the whole lifetime of the masses into labour-time.
> —KARL MARX, *CAPITAL*

"It's my turn to speak," announces Angel, the twenty-seven-year-old math
teacher in Ramona Diaz's documentary *The Learning*, to get the attention of her classroom of young African American men. She wants to show
them a video of her trip to Disneyland, a far cry from the complex geometric formulae she makes them memorize for class. The video was certainly not part of any math lesson she was hired for. She begins by saying
that her dream even as a poor girl in the outskirts of Manila was to go to
Disneyland, and she wants to share her recent first visit with them. As a
way to encourage the students to talk about their aspirations, she recounts
her reaction to a stage production at the amusement park, in which an
evil witch threatened to steal the characters' dreams. After showing the
video, the documentary cuts back to her in front of the classroom, saying, "I believe that dreams will come true, then it happened. I am here.
I am with you. I am teaching you." Oddly, being "here," her arrival in the
classroom as a math teacher with the young men, or even her arrival into
the United States, was not her dream at all. She said so quite plainly in
introducing her video: Visiting Disneyland was her actual dream as a little
girl. Being in a US classroom was her family's dream, the viewer later finds
out, not hers. Indeed, Angel's situation as the embodiment of other
people's and nations' economic dreams stems from the historical violence
of imperialism and from neoliberal state solutions for systemic racial inequities in underserved school districts.

   In narrating the stories of Filipina teachers working in predominantly
Black school systems, *The Learning* stages the physical adjacency of two
sets of racialized bodies linking two historical trajectories, slavery and co-

lonialism, and connected by the operations of American white settler empire. At the outset of the documentary, the film flashes a quick text-book account of the beginning of US colonial education in the Philippines. In 1901, after the bloody Philippine-American War, the first American Thomasites, named after the ship USS *Thomas* that brought them, ar-rived on Philippine shores. These American teachers were recruited from all over the United States to teach the natives of the new island possession. The Philippine-American War had by then starved or killed thousands of Filipinos, and the arrival of American teachers was to pave over the devastation to prepare Filipino children for their new nation under US rule. The documentary captures the tides turning back.

The continuing decrease in teachers' salaries and resources for public schools across the United States, especially in communities of color, over the past few decades has compelled some states to recruit from abroad, including the Philippines, in an effort to cut costs for the districts while providing much needed staff.[1] In 2001, the punitive and unfunded No Child Left Behind Act promulgated by the George W. Bush administra-tion forced many school districts to hire Filipinos, once under American colonial tutelage, to serve as science, math, and special education teach-ers in under-resourced, predominantly Black and immigrant school dis-tricts. The act mandated schools to meet federal standards of academic achievement or risk losing federal funding, but the government provided no resources for already underfunded and failing school systems. Ninety thousand overseas-trained teachers were sought by the United States in the first decade of this century from the Philippines, India, Jamaica, and Spain.[2] Filipinos arrived in one hundred school districts across the United States. At the time of filming in 2006, about six hundred, or 10 percent, of Baltimore's school district teachers were from the Philippines. An army of foreign, racially distinct workers from a former colony and tutelary, cli-ent state arrive to ameliorate the race and class inequities in the United States caused by a history of slavery and past de jure and current de facto segregation. State policies that continue to privatize solutions for class and race inequities, like No Child Left Behind, facilitated such a meeting of two spaces and two historical trajectories to address race and the global economic inequities of liberal capitalism.

The Learning follows the inaugural school year of Filipina teachers re-cruited from the Philippines to teach in Baltimore's struggling, predom-inantly Black public schools.[3] What is striking about the documentary is the number of scenes dedicated to the moments of the teachers singing and dancing with students or other teachers, nine in total across the ninety-minute film. Diaz deploys the observational and participatory modes with interviews and classroom scenes with her subjects, though she herself is absent from the frame.[4] Diaz attributes the abundance of these often joyful scenes as the condition of filming the Filipinas' social everyday at home and work.[5] On the one hand, these intentional performances in the film's narrative complement the conventional interviews Diaz conducts with the women and the scenes of the women at work. They are not simply illustrative of the explanatory power of the film's formal interviews. Instead, they offer a glimpse of the negotiations, contestations, and production of the affective proximities demanded of and embodied by the teachers. On the other hand, I argue the larger point that the performative qualities of Diaz's filmmaking, her editing and her various framings of the women's bodies in motion, provide texture to these scenes of arrival (in the classroom, in the hometown, in their bodies) at key moments in the narrative to account for effects of their living and working across social histories and worlds beyond their contracted roles as teachers and export labor.

"Arrival" in Tagalog is *dating* (dah-TEENG), but the word also describes the impact or force a person or object brings to a social milieu. The Philippine writer-critic Bienvenido Lumbera defines *dating* as "*ang impresyong iniiwan sa isang tao na pagmumukha, bihis, pananalita at kilos ng isang indibidwal* [the impression left on a person by someone's appearance, dress, address, and movement]."[6] *Dating* alludes to the aesthetic qualities of a person that leave a mark on another. Lumbera applies this definition to literary works to describe the effects of art works that place object or performance and audience in relationship to one other.

> *Pag nahaharap tayo sa isang likhang-sining, sa ganyan ding paraan pumapasok sa ating kamalayan ang mga katangiang umaakit na magustuhan o ayawan natin ang trabaho ng manlilikha. Ang isang painting, tugtugin, o pagtatanghal ay dumarating sa audience na nakaabang, parang destinasyon sa isang paglalakbay, sa magaganap na kamalayan nito. Ang kaganapan ng pagsapit ng likha, ang dating ng likha, nagbibitiw ang audience ng pahayag ng pagkatuwa, pagkasaya o paghanga.*
>
> [When we encounter a work of art, the qualities that make us like or dislike the artist's work enter our consciousness in this manner. A painting, a piece of music, or a stage play reaches the consciousness of the audience, which awaits like a destination in a journey. At the moment of the work's impact, its arrival compels the audience to outbursts of laughter, joy, or admiration.][7]

Using the root definition of *dating* as an occasion of arrival, Lumbera expands the understanding of arrival to its very conditions of possibility. The concept includes the affective pathway, a journey (*paglalakbay*), from expressive art work to receiver that traces the movement of artistic qualities to the consciousness of the observer or listener. As the literary critic David Bayot elaborates in his reading of Lumbera: "The word has the denotation and connotation of both appeal and impact."[8] *Dating* as the movement and impact of an object or performance, its animating force, might be understood as the aesthetics of the artistic expression. In this spatial movement from object to observer, Lumbera deploys visual as well as haptic sensorial indicators to describe how the expressive work reaches out, reaches, and leaves "impressions" on the observer's consciousness and elicits bodily "outbursts" (*pahayag*).

Arrival as a multifaceted opening is an occasion that disrupts but also makes visible vital interactions with and ways to apprehend a potent figure and her symbolic possibility. In informal conversation, when someone is noticed for her bearing in a social setting, she is said to possess *dating*.[9] For example, when a person is said to "make an entrance," she is able to redirect the flow of time and the shape of the social space. Benedict Anderson explains in his now-classic essay that this potency in the Javanese context, distinguishing Power with a capital *P* from Western notions of power with a small *p*,

> emphasizes the sign of Power's concentration, not the demonstration of its exercise or use. These signs are looked for both in the person of the Power holder and in the society in which he wields Power. The two are, of course, intimately related. In the words of Indonesia's most prominent contemporary intellectual, "A central concept in the Javanese traditional view of life is the direct relationship between the state of a person's inner self and his capacity to control the environment."[10]

For Anderson, environment, observer, and power holder are all intimately tied together in this ecology of potency. Order and harmony in the surroundings are the manifestation of a person's power. Orderliness, it is assumed, issues from the person who holds power. The power holder should not be seen to exert effort in showing she has power, but rather the signs of power should be apparent in the control and order found in the environment over which she presides. One says of a person, *malakas ang dating niya* (her/his/their *dating* is powerful). I would note that the attribution of *dating* is not limited to beauty queens, celebrities, and public figures but extends to any person in any social setting.

Dating is often associated with men, hence the use of *malakas* (strong) to describe its intensity rather than just quality. While this Southeast Asian concept of potency and communal personhood is implicitly gendered male, I shift the focus of this vernacular onto the female subjects of the documentary film to illustrate how Diaz's framing and cuts alongside the women's bodily presentations as teachers generate and deploy *dating* to order relations and their surroundings. This affective energy while indexing the encounter between object, person, or performance and audience also generates a feel to the space and relationships between and among people. While *dating* suggests a distancing relation, it also names a way of knowing, relating, and, most importantly, sensing the person or object through that distance. The person's qualities, her *dating*, conjoin her to the observer. In *dating*, aesthetics is bound to corporeality and communality to index localized pathways, openings, networks, and textures that make a space habitable and time sensible with others on the occasion of someone's arrival. Ascribed to persons, *dating* is not necessarily about being conventionally beautiful but having social potency, which English words like "attractive," "captivating," or "prepossessing" only in part suggest. Those possible equivalents suggest gathering of energies to a focal point or centripetal force. As the root of "centripetal" implies, center-seeking forces like attraction capture and cumulate attention. By contrast, *dating* names how a body or object exudes centrifugal force, negative or positive, in a locale. While compelling notice might be an effect, *dating* more significantly issues out from the body to the space around it and circulates within that space. Like centripetal attraction, centrifugal *dating* comes in various intensities. One "feels" the person in the room. Perhaps others notice when a person enters a room. Perhaps, in moving about the room or in speaking, others take extra note of the person. Reconsidering aesthetics in *The Difference Aesthetic Makes*, Kandice Chuh returns to Aristotle's notion of *sensus communis*, common sense, which "actively referred to corporeality—to that which enables the specific senses (sight, hearing, touch and smell) to coordinate syncretically what each distinctively perceives."[11] I read common sense here with the emphasis on the localized space of communing generated by the moment of sensory encounter at the moment of arrival or performance. Taking this cue from Chuh, this shared space of feeling that an entity's "arrival" elicits is a way to apprehend the object as well as the particular space and moment that the receiver shares with others. From this sensory foundation, I underscore the fusing of the word's conventional root as "arrival" and the relationships outward occasioned by that arrival to condition space and sociality.

Beyond charisma, as a positive attribute, *dating* is a form of nonverbal address that gives pleasure as it defines and generates the terms of collectivity. A person's *dating*, or "appeal and impact," to use Bayot's phrase, creates conditions for sociality and communal emergence.[12] A person might even be unaware of her *dating*, but she is admired usually by way of group acknowledgment, so individuals might be bonded through admiration of the person as achieved state, creating a temporary sociality. The anthropologist Fenella Cannell has described how beauty in Filipino cultural practices, such as gay beauty pageants, is a form of communal power, not only in the act of holding the crowd's attention but also in making a social network manifest and visible through audience acclamation.[13] Thus beauty, or better, *biyuti* as the queer vernacularization of the English word, defines personhood, as Martin Manalansan has argued, as opposed to individual or identity, to underscore its social imbrication to encompass communal and historical configurations.[14] Self-presentation emerges from tactical deployments of social scripts and situations within localized settings. Therefore *biyuti* as the manifestation of personhood beyond personal appearance comes to light only *in communality*.

Dating is relational and communal in queer and feminist terms. Given this flow among bodies and environment, *dating* is the effect of reshaping time and place for communal pleasure and to create the conditions of sociality and imagine another order together. Extending Cannell's discussion on beauty and Manalansan's on *biyuti*, I argue that a person's *dating* as arrival and emergence is a tactile, and sometimes tactical, redirection of time and space. What emerge in arrival understood as engroupment are the immaterial forces that circulate to create the terms of the local community and its legibility to itself. Ruminating on *dating*, I suggest that *dating* as affect describes the interruptive spaces and time within global migration by which overseas Filipinas order their worlds; craft their own departures, returns, and arrivals; mark the chronic textures of their habitation; and gesture to other worlds.

"When You Wish upon a Star," or *Dating* as Embodied Journeys

> Like a bolt out of the blue / Suddenly, it comes to you / When you wish upon a star / Your dreams come true / When a star is born / They possess a gift or two / One of them is this
> "When You Wish Upon a Star," from Disney's *Pinocchio*

At the end of the school year, Angel stages the coming together of two racialized and classed groups forged from violent histories of dispossession when she choreographs a Filipino poetry and dance performance for a school assembly. The camera pans from the ground up, accompanied by the echo of heels striding confidently down the hallway, then to Angel, who appears in a full-length, bright pink dress with distinctive Filipina butterfly sleeves. The frame flashes a poster, "Harlem Park Family Highlighting the Filipino Culture"; cheers rise in the background. The camera cuts to a Black young man dressed in a white shirt and a colorful neckerchief, suggesting a Filipino farmer's outfit. He recites "I Am a Filipino," a poem by the Filipina-American poet Ruth Mabanglo, which takes the perspective of an overseas Filipina who hopes to preserve her stories through her children even in diaspora. Facing the audience, the young man reads into the microphone, "And this is what I will teach / My children: / You must return to your roots / Despite the wounds; / You must know the legend / Of your brown skin; / You must direct your zeal / And harness your dreams / In recognizing the past / In the stored memories, / In your desired goals." Mabanglo's words, voiced by the student, speak to dreams and legends as one teacher's desires and the next generation's inheritance.

The young man's voice becomes the voiceover as the documentary cuts to Angel dancing with four Black female students wearing Filipino embroidered blouses or butterfly-sleeved dresses like Angel's. With lights dimmed, they dance the "Pandanggo sa Ilaw," fandango of lights, a popular lowland Christian folk dance. Dancers balance and swirl small candles on their heads and the back of their hands or palms to simulate fireflies twinkling in the evening. The dance is a jaunty crowd pleaser; the string music picks up speed, and the dancers perform ever more impressive balancing feats with the lights. It is a playful dance that elicits and is egged on by the "oohs," "ahhs," and rhythmic claps of audience members, who are also anxious about the possibility of candles or dancers faltering. The dance is always a great finale for any repertoire, including here. The final forceful strum hits, and the dancers strike a triumphant pose, a Philippine flag unfurls, and the audience cheers in adulation. The dancers laugh in appreciation and in congratulation of one another's well-choreographed teamwork. The performance is a visual and bodily reminder of the creative communing outside the curriculum that must and does transpire in the classroom as a work place.

Whether in Angel teaching rhythmic mnemonics for geometric formulae or in teaching songs, poems, and dances that students don't quite understand fully, these are communal habitations of time and bodies that have multiple and unpredictable effects. The familiar rhythm and resonance of brown skins, loss of home, dreams, legends, memories, and aspiration serve as corporeal mnemonics to marginalized histories and racialized bodies compelled to live alongside one another. Here, in bringing historical effects and journeys together, I underscore the idea of resonance rather than equivalence. Mabanglo, a Filipina-American poet residing in Hawaii, ends her diasporic poem with a placeless, timeless, soul: "I am a Filipino with a soul / That will remain Filipino / In whatever Country, / In Whatever time / In whatever body." The "soul" that capital seeks to capitalize, as Berardi has observed, is given iterative and itinerant life in this migration. The Filipino "soul" inhabits other bodies, times, and places, in this case a young Black man in Baltimore. In the privatized and managed transnational teacher exchange, each racialized and underdeveloped community—cheap Filipina labor and under-resourced Black districts—is supposed to solve the economic and social needs of the other. Angel and her students share bodily and poetic rhythms, and Diaz's cuts make apparent the painful resonance but also the unaccounted joy between different racialized histories of containment and violence.

Diaz splices this exhilarating celebratory scene between one teacher worrying about mounting debts in the Philippines and another apprehensive about her classroom performance review. Angel's scene of terpsichorean balancing with students serves as a counterpoint to the scenes of quantitative valuation that come before and after. Notably, both surrounding scenes are about the violent monetization of the teachers' professional but intrinsically qualitative human and creative activity, quantitative assessments on which their economic future hangs in the balance. With the scene of reciprocal joy making in poetry and dance, the documentary thus interrupts the reductive quantitative narrative of debt and remittance to the Philippines and of workplace evaluations in the United States. That is, the film entwines dance and poetry in a narrative thread about the disciplinary power to which the women are subject, a power that emanates from both national spaces and operates through material and abstract inequities in terms of race, color, gender, and class.

When Angel talks to her class about the various dreams she had as a young girl in the Philippines, she concludes, "Then it happened." The ambiguous "it" that "happened" was that Angel had been transformed into and would alone bear the weight of her family's dream within a remittance economy. Remittance is the promise of a future elsewhere and her whole lifetime traded for a family's future. In a later scene, a group of teachers gather for a party and make up a song about paychecks that disappear as quickly as they receive them. The song about hard work, "I am not sad here / As long as they're happy," makes an unconvincing case that other family members' happiness elsewhere makes up for their own toil, trouble, sadness, and time expended for those paychecks. The film then cuts to staff from a remittance agency cheerfully greeting the teachers. They appear every payday to transmit these checks that quantify pain, joy, and effort into an amount sent to families. One teacher says that she counts biweekly or monthly paydays to make the time go faster. She marks time by the cycles of paydays remaining before she can go home to her family in the summer. The teachers' emotions are deferred ("I am not sad here"), since those are saved, much like the money, for the family an ocean and a number of pay cycles away. The feel of time and feeling itself are translated and quantified into their money equivalent.

This financial and emotional burden of embodying rather than having a dream is apparent in Angel's return home. Her scene of return opens with her back to the camera in front of a money exchange booth. Framed by the iron bars of the booth, the young teacher exchanges two thousand dollars for Philippine pesos to spend on her visit to her family in the humble outskirts of Manila. In the next scene, her extended family goes on a grocery shopping spree. She can barely contain her frustration and her pocketbook as she tries to restrain the various family members' buying frenzy, who are impulsively throwing spaghetti sauce, blocks of cheese, and other items into the shopping cart. The items keep piling up despite her repeated pleas of "just one," "we already bought that," "I already brought you gifts." The ritual gift upon return home (*pasalubong*) is not enough; the returnee must also provide the opportunity for the family to consume some more.

Angel's status obligation is tied intimately to gift giving, redistribution of wealth, and family demands. She is expected to pay for the hundreds of dollars of groceries as part of the celebration to mark her return home. The ability to consume is the pleasure the family is after, not necessarily the objects themselves. This provision of both the pleasure of shopping and the acquisition of goods is her duty as the primary breadwinner for the family.[15] Angel is trapped in an insatiable exchange: She must continually convert her labor and time away from family into money, which is then used to reproduce family ties via cash remittance and the purchase of goods to address material lack as well as "make up" for time lost at home. Earlier in the film, while greeting her family on a social media platform, she asks, "Pa, how are you?" Her father replies glibly to the query about his state of health or well-being, "Waiting for your paycheck." While meant as a joke, the teasing carries for Angel the disciplinary reminder of her duties and debt of obligation. Her father's and family's well-being anticipates cash remittance as evidence of her commitment and emotional ties.

At a family meeting after the shopping scene, the mom happily cries, "All of our hardships have been exchanged for a better life. I had prayed to go from rags to riches. I really thank God for that." Angel's father adds for the camera, "She's taken over my responsibilities as a father," exclaiming how Angel is a godsend, for whom they "prayed twenty-seven years." The scene is supposed to be touching, a heartfelt expression of love and appreciation in front of the cameras. However, the mood changes once Angel speaks, taking the role foisted upon her as head of the family:

> Now let's talk about how we will go about this. How we will accomplish what we want together. What my expectations are of you and what you expect from me. We all have to work to go from rags to riches, not just me. Because I cannot do it alone. Honestly, I cannot . . . I can't be the only one to work for all of you . . . I also want you to know that I have my own life.

Angel adamantly refuses the role so that she might define another trajectory for her absence and work. She also refuses the easy characterization of her as savior, dutiful daughter, and head of the family. Angel does not so much reject filial and fiscal responsibility as remind the others of the collective nature of this "debt of obligation."

Angel thus seeks to recalibrate and reshift the burden of this debt of obligation as a collective effort rather than an individuated one: "When I go to America, it's not to buy everything that you want. We all have to work to go from rags to riches, not just me. I cannot do it alone," she exclaims to her family. Debt of obligation, as Sarita See explains in her reading of Bulosan's short story "Magno Rubio," is another "economy of debt that is based on assumptions of reciprocity, generosity and collective survival."[16] As a sociality, this system of obligation in its ideal form is often invoked for communal good. However, in practice gendered inequities, including marital status, sexuality, reproductive capacity, family status obligations, and the global labor market, work to distribute unevenly the burden of survival and social reproduction on women. As an unmarried and childless daughter, Angel is obligated to help the family. On the national level, her youth and education are cultivated and marketed by the Philippine state to be exported in the global market for social reproductive labor. The scene could be construed as Angel redefining her role in the family upon her arrival. However, this redefinition is not redirection at all. Her plea still holds her family as the structure defining the terms of negotiation and obligation. Indeed, the lack of response from the family as the camera scans the faces in the room for a reaction to her is telling in her attempt to renegotiate the terms of her "debt of obligation."

Thus when Angel pronounces at the end of her earlier video "lesson" "I am here. I am with you," the declarative ambiguity could take on a different valence in terms of being "here" and "with" the students in locational proximity. She may not only be referring to her presence in the classroom but to the class watching her arrival at her fantasy space away from both places of confinement. When Angel introduces the film to her class, the documentary cuts to Angel watching the video with the class, her back to Diaz's camera. She then looks back at the camera, at the imaginary viewer, every so often smiling with pride and delight. She gets emotional watching herself, wiping away a tear on cue as she listens to her own voiceover about tearing up over a witch taking away Donald Duck's dreams.

> [Cut to Angel watching the video] It really strikes my heart. I started to cry without me knowing, as the tears were already falling down onto my cheeks. I can't imagine that I was able to reach my dreams. Because we're just poor; we didn't have the means. [Cut to Disney video] But because I tried my very best, one by one, I am starting to reach all my goals and all my dreams in life. When I went here to America, it is also my dream to be here.

The film cuts from the vacation video to Angel watching the video to Angel speaking to the class. The cut to the vacation video shows her sashaying down Disneyland's Main Street, not the United States itself but a distilled version of it. She is heard saying on the video, "See! This is so beautiful. This is Wonderland!" She makes a half-turn back to the video camera as if in a model photo shoot, her coat flaring out, taking a moment to smile into the video camera as if to exclaim, I'm here! Then she turns away, jauntily walking along the pathway toward her Wonderland. Diaz plays with dizzying but smooth cuts and cross-cuts when Angel shows her dream video to the class.

In the film image, *dating* as sensory reach may be represented when the desired object appears on screen, as in Angel's close up, camera gaze, and slow motion. Time slows or is even arrested, and space is reshaped in this reorientation. Yet rather than think of the film medium recreating the feeling of *dating*, Angel and Diaz here take cinematic cues already found across the vacation video, the classroom, and the documentary camera to craft Angel's coming into her own. In layering her film cuts, Diaz mixes places and times to signal and extend Angel's moment of ecstatic pleasure in the vacation video and in the documentary itself as she rewatches the video. Ecstatic in the etymological sense of being outside oneself, classroom Angel chuckles to herself and revels in Disneyworld Angel delighting in those moments on mythical Main Street. At times, Diaz's documentary tells the larger teacher story, but other times the point of view is Angel's looking out at the camera. Then both classroom Angel and Disneyland Angel look out to Diaz's camera and its audience. The frame within a frame and the juxtaposed images are as giddy-making as Angel's own state: Donald Duck, Disney, fuzzy videos, the math classroom, and the continual glances at the camera to reach out of the documentary. Only in this complex layering can Diaz make visual Angel's *dating*, the potency she projects beyond herself into her immediate classroom audience and her audience-yet-to-be. Perhaps between the cuts the viewer catches a glimpse of Angel traversing the pathway, always about to arrive.

Doubling over and over, she weeps with laughter for the camera while watching and reliving that moment of arrival into her fantasy world, outside of time. Angel shows the class and Diaz *her* "dream world" and "bodily state." She is beside herself. In the doubled glances at the camera toward a real and imagined audience, Angel frames and makes a spectacle of herself, so to speak, making public a personal and emotional world. Angel also invokes her moment of arrival, her *dating*, at which she gets choked up once again. That moment of being beside herself offers a glimpse of transformation and of other possible selves for Angel. She creates the environment by acknowledging the imagined audience of both cameras with inchoate glances, glimpses, and knowing looks. Acknowledgment here in looking at the vacation video camera and at Diaz's camera to show her delight is a communal act that frames her persona outside the classroom and an imagined group-yet-to-be at once; it calls up another space, one decidedly neither her impoverished part of Manila nor the inner-city Baltimore she shares with her students. While Disneyworld is imbricated within capitalism's branding fantasy, for Angel, her arrival "here" is not bound to her (Filipino) family's financial wants or to her (American) students' educational needs; it is instead a representation of desires away from both to which she brings students *with* her. Another reality is activated. Doubled ad infinitum in the jumble of juxtaposed images, Angel watching herself with her students, looking into the camera while looking back at us, marks the immeasurable pleasure in the vanishing moment, perhaps even a "bolt from the blue," of recognition of another self in another world even as it marks its impossibility.

"I've Never Been to Me," or *Dating* as Refusing Redemption

> Hey lady, you lady, cursin' at your life / You're a discontented mother
> and a regimented wife / I've no doubt you dream about the things
> you never do / But I wish someone had talked to me / Like I wanna
> talk to you
>
> "I've Never Been to Me," Charlene

The documentary film ends with Dorotea, a beloved veteran school-
teacher of twenty-seven years, singing the Charlene ballad "I've Never
Been to Me" at a local karaoke joint during the summer return to her pro-
vincial hometown. The camera closes up on Dorotea's sweat-soaked but
composed face as she sings in Filipino-accented English. The reverb on
the karaoke machine is too high and overwhelms her voice, but this does
not deter the forty-something mother of four from emoting the wistful
words weighed down with regret, recollection, and nostalgia. Her body
commands the space, and she contorts her face with more intensity than
the viewer had seen from her in front of the classroom earlier in the film.
It is the height of the humid, wet season in Ormoc, a small rural town
amid a cluster of islands in the Visayas, Philippines, far from metropoli-
tan Manila and even farther from her work place in inner-city Baltimore.
White plastic chairs, serviceable but dirty from years of rain, heat, and
casual wiping, surround Dorotea in the open-air karaoke bar that Diaz
has set for her emergence into the global stage.

In editing the film, Diaz chooses "I've Never Been to Me" as the coda
for all the women, the 1977 ballad made famous (or infamous) by Charlene.[17] Dorotea's rendition of the plaintive ballad accompanies a visual
montage of all the women spending time with their families for the summer. Diaz thematizes and asserts their presence in their hometowns, albeit in a wistful lament. The initial poignancy in closing a documentary
film about export labor with this song lies in the migrant women's negotiation with places, bodies, and times out of sync with family's expectations and their own aspirations. The ballad stages an encounter between
the female speaker, who has traveled the world, and another who has chosen to stay in the small town. The wistful narrator entreats the other to
find meaningful life back home as her own seemingly glamorous, globe-
trotting life has not yielded happiness. Despite travels around the world,
the one place the speaker has never been, as the song refrain goes, is to
"me." By leaving home, she has left herself in the process. Recollection,
regret, and return define this "me"—a destination rendered impossible.

"Me" becomes place, body, affect, and temporality all at once. The song's "me" is a continually deferred place and time that neither speaker nor addressee has yet realized. "I have never been to me" in this context thus points to an impossibility whereby the women cannot fully narrate themselves out of nation-state economic logics—as income earners for the Philippines and bodies that cover over the contradiction of income and race inequality in the United States.

While the documentary begins ostensibly to tell a story about race relations and social reproduction, in my interview with the director, Diaz described her film about the daily lives of the migrant teachers as partly about the women "coming into their own."[18] While filming, her intention was to follow the lives of the women over one school year. After filming that year in the classrooms and homes of the women, Diaz's editing process forged another narrative arc, the trope of the return home. At this editing stage, the film transformed from one primarily about reproductive labor to one about staging physical returns of the women to their families in the Philippines. Diaz's last-minute decision to follow the women's summer return home to the Philippines provided her footage during editing with, as she described, "golden moments" for the "third act" of the documentary. Notably, all the women refuse the terms of their return to their families, each one insisting on redefining their relationship to marriage, family, and their home town: The younger Angel puts her foot down with her family, Dorotea visits her old school to reclaim her place in it, and Rhea breaks up with her husband in the prison where he is being held. While providing a sense of closure and completion for the narratives, the returns are also a way to stage the women's transformation as they "come into their own."[19] Thus Diaz set out a challenge for herself and her film. The documentary sought both to record the women's everyday negotiation with cultural conflicts while caring for families abroad and also to capture the subject's emergence, "coming into their own," outside of both constraints. In one sense, this traces a triumphalist arc in which the women's return home would serve in part as a redemptive moment for the dislocated care workers.

Much Filipino-American and diasporic literature, not just scholarship, takes return, figuratively or literally, as one of its thematic concerns.[20] I would argue that focusing (only) on the perhaps inevitably failed returns home recenters and recites once again the ideological power of nation, family, employment, and sentimentality as primary sites of social and identity formation. Return is indeed a function of desire but might be mandatory and enforced for some and even impossible for many, as is the case for undocumented and overstaying Filipinos around the world.[21] In a study of a Filipino community in Daly City, California, Benito Vergara asserts that "re-turn" can more complicatedly take the form of

> repeated turning . . . through political activism, assertions of ethnic pride, nostalgia, consumerism or just vague remembering. Re-turn is obliquely opposed to the narrative of assimilation. The tension between this remembrance and the demands of citizenship in the new homeland, the obligations in different directions, constitute a predicament for the Philippine immigrant.[22]

While productively expanding return's possibilities, the repeated turning once again privileges the nation-state as dictating the terms of the continual pivots even in resisting its power.

Return intimates looping back not just to the Philippines in most cases but also a recovery of lost time and relationships. Return brings the tension of belonging caught between national and familial continuity and the fear of the impossibility of recovery of the past.[23] The fantasy of continuity assumes static subjects and relationships in the homeland, and the purported breaks assume the erasure or at least disavowal of contiguous histories. Furthermore, for my purposes here, these desires are premised on the overvaluation of the individual as an autonomous agent rather than as always already integrated in a social network of people, histories, and multiple and ever-changing desires. By shifting the viewing frame from one of return home to iterations of arrival, *dating* would disrupt this chronology. At each occasion of arrival, the one who returns configures the localized space and relationships around and beyond her anew. As with Angel showing her video of Disneyland, arrival or *dating* may be thought of as an interruption of narrative expectations and a way of taking space and inhabiting time by the very act of entry into a communal setting.

In the scene before her karaoke singing, Diaz shows Dorotea on her visit back to her old school. Fellow teachers and students alike welcome her to the school with exuberant tears of delight. Banners outside the school grounds announce her return from "Maryland, USA," and upon entering a classroom, the students politely stand in ceremony to greet her in unison as they would a visiting guest: "Good morning, Mrs. Godinez." Recognizing the polite ritual, she admonishes playfully in English, "I am not a visitor, I am a *balikbayan* [returnee]." This felt need for a reminder underscores how the categories "visitor" and "*balikbayan*" are not only two distinct subjects but denote two different entry points for the subject into the local community. The visitor does not share a past with the community, but Dorotea as *balikbayan* comes to claim the past and the present as if it were not so much an unbroken chain but an unwieldy one. However, from her family's and students' perspective she is indeed coming for a temporary summer visit, only to break physical ties with them once again. The summer's end will repeat the sad and equally tearful farewell shown at the beginning of the film.

Given the intertwined personal and national histories across spaces, accounting for the experience of migration might be better understood in its complexity not simply as a spatial movement but also a temporal one, resulting in conflicting selves and desires.[24] While the students' polite gesture figures the encounter as a meeting of two spaces ("Maryland, USA," as the welcome banner announces, and Ormoc, Philippines), Dorotea figures her return as reconnecting shared history, tenuously stitched in the interim by remittances, phone calls, and other communication media. What was her beloved classroom for twenty-seven years received her as a celebrated guest, but a guest, nonetheless, who no longer shares the space, to be sure, but also seems to erase a shared past as a term of belonging. What Dorotea hears in the polite greeting and gesture is the "harsh sentence" that Ranajit Guha elaborates in his essay "The Migrant's Time": "You no longer belong here; you're no longer one of us."[25] Guha explains that "the displacement is made all the more poignant by the paradox that it corresponds to no distantiation in time. For it is stapled firmly to an accentuated and immediate present cut off from a shared past by the adverbial force of 'no longer.'"[26] In Dorotea's case, the break was not one of willed abandonment of home and family. As a recruited worker and *balikbayan* she did not run away for the glamorous life, like the song's narrator, although that might be projected on her by those she left behind. Rather, compelled labor migration was one way to keep her family together toward a different future.

With this corrective scene in mind, Dorotea's rendition of the song is not simply about return. Rather, the speaker and listener might be read as possible versions of the other in time, one going on a global sojourn and the other trapped in localized longing. As an admonition, the song sets up a simultaneity of selves, since the speaker claims a shared past as well as an alternative possibility with the addressee, as if to say that you are what I was and you are what I could have been: "I can see so much of me still living in your eyes." By doing so, the speaker brings together in one narrative two timelines and two selves. Just as important, the ballad form pulls at the audience's heartstrings to connect not only the two suffering figures but also the singer and her audience. The song's plaint dramatizes the scene of return for Dorotea's (and the other women's) homecoming in the song's implied narrative of exile and return. The song thus nuances Dorotea's insistence on naming the terms of her return a few minutes earlier in the film. What the song asserts is her dispersed place but also the multiple temporalities shared with the listener, both the present and past, to be sure, but also possible futures.

The ballad's plaintive note preserves the chronic tension of spatial dispersal and plural embodied temporalities. This bodily and affective index captures Dorotea insisting on a script that wrestles with multiple entanglements over and against one that may be unitarily proscribed by the filmmaker as a return, or the Philippines as "home," or the United States as racialized workplace. The words sung by Dorotea become a teaching moment to define herself and her place to the karaoke addressee, her family, friends, acquaintances—not only the viewer.[27] When Dorotea sings "I've never been to me" to move her (imagined) hometown audience, she provides a response to a fantasy projection of glamour accumulated through travel abroad. The song choice does not so much reject the circuits of travel but the meaning of that circulation. The painfully clichéd talking interlude signals disillusionment: "Hey, you know what paradise is? It's a lie / A fantasy we create about people and places as we'd like them to be." Paradise here may be redefined not so much about a place elsewhere. Instead it is a concept fueled by false expectations from both national sites and promises. Thus, the alienation of self that the song rejects is actually the burden of representation hoisted upon both her and the other women's returning bodies.

In that moment, Dorotea would have command of the room and these evocations, to call together a community not only in her hometown but with the other women in the film and the viewing audience from film to global stage. Her *dating* in her karaoke performance orients her body and the viewer elsewhere beyond the vocabulary of economic exchange that makes up the false "paradise." The karaoke performance produces not just proximity but propinquity, or fellow feeling, and affinity with the audience.[28] I want to distinguish proximity from propinquity. That is, to be proximate does not necessarily mean affinity. To be next to someone does not guarantee connection, but to have propinquity is to produce a sense of shared connection. The production of such affinities is part of the "creative labor," as Lucy Burns has put it, of these performances.[29] Here, I underscore that creative labor may be understood as part of but also distinct from reproductive labor. It is a creative capacity wrested from labor-time. Propinquity, or fellow feeling, with the audience limns out the outlines of community, a *sensus communis*, from which the subjects emerge.

The cultural critic and scholar Patrick Flores's exploration of *palabas* (a show, movie, or stage play) is helpful in thinking through shared or common sense. Flores mines the term *palabas*, which can also mean the interplay of emotional display (for example, crying) and staged performance:

> *Palabas* is spectacle and appearance. It speaks of an outward thrust from an interior, and so is both inclination and intimation (*saloobin*). There is a deliberate agency at work in a gesture of performance or the process of making something appear and making it appear in a particular way (*papalabasin* or *pinapalabas*). It may be construed as modern to the degree that it is reflexive, a mediated exposition (a cognate of *pakitang tao* [self-presentation]) in relation to a premeditated exposure: it is theater and it involves acting, diversion, pedagogy. It is (dis)guise and it is manifestation.[30]

Flores goes through the permutations and nuances of the word that at its etymological root signals the movement *toward* exteriority, *pa-* denoting that shared movement from subject to audience, as Lumbera and Bayot's reading of *dating*. Flores's "outward thrust" in defining *palabas* suggests the directionality (inclination) and force of a performance, whether on stage or in everyday life. *Palabas*, as self-presentation, is not necessarily deception or lying meant to fulfill some ulterior motive. *Palabas* is the controlled manifestation of emotion for social purposes.

I bring up the translational nuances not to argue that Filipinos necessarily confuse everyday emotion with the stage but to signal that for any emotional expression there is a real or imagined audience, thus suggesting a creative space even if constrained by external circumstances. Dorotea's karaoke performance, like other staged performances, targets outward to her hometown audience, one acquainted with the form, vernacular, and repertoire of songs. As Christine Balance argues, "Pinoys do not simply perform karaoke. Instead, they teach, learn, remember, and invoke particular memories and ways of life to the shared language of pop music."[31] Such tropical renditions, to use Balance's phrase, are judged more for the general mood the singer is able to create in the room than for the actual words or content, which may only be superficially heard. Perhaps the audience hears only the names of various European cities, which evoke faraway places, and the refrain "I have never been to me," naming some vague sentiment.

Dorotea's series of gestures, pleas, and wails create an atmosphere and mood in the room where she is the center of attention. *Dating* generates value in atmosphere and event as ends in themselves. Let us recall once again Lumbera's description of arrival as event: "Ang kaganapan ng pagsapit ng likha, *ang dating ng likha, nagbibitiw ang audience ng pahayag ng pagkatuwa, pagkasaya o paghanga. [At the experience of the artwork's impact,* its arrival compels the audience to react with laughter, joy, or admiration.]"[32] Dorotea affirms not only the audience but also asserts her relation and proper place in that community. I would thus connect arrival to futurity in the fullness of present possibility. If return is framed as an iteration of arrival, the past as a discrete temporal comparison recedes. That is, return is not so much about a turn to the past but its reframing.

Arrival or *dating* is an experience in itself. Rather than the "fantasy production" of global capitalism, *dating* as a disruptive event is possibility itself.[33] While the summer visit accomplishes physical proximity, the work to create connections happens in these spaces. This sort of labor exchange is part of such acts of returning home: an affective negotiation that includes making place and atmosphere to stage and map herself and her entanglements in dispersed and scattered ways—and to imagine another geography of self and belonging.

"I Will Survive," or *Dating* as Unproductive World Making

> And you see me / Somebody new / I'm not that chained up little person / Still in love with you
>
> "I Will Survive," Gloria Gaynor

Rhea, a special education teacher, drives home after her class determined to "move on," she says, from her husband in the Philippines. Moving on did not just mean leaving him in the Philippines to take the job abroad or even the permanent separation from him that Diaz shows in the film. Beside the act of migration, moving on in Rhea's self-help language was her redirection of care. "In the Philippines, my car was second hand. Here, I want a brand-new car. I work so hard here," she proclaims and then adds, "My joy this time." Armed with endless self-help mantras and advice, Rhea struggles with her abusive husband, who has landed in prison in the Philippines for selling drugs. She speaks with him on the phone: "The mind is very powerful. . . . If you always think negative, it all comes back to you." Immediately the film cuts to a Zumba session with her friends at her apartment.

> (Rhea voiceover): I have a very different outlook now. He's there. But I accept that this is my reality. This is his reality. I can't do anything about it. I can only make sure that everyday I am happy. I don't think it's being selfish. It's just about being fair to myself. I started taking

care of myself more than I did before. I'm thinking I should look beautiful. If I feel good, everything will be good.

Rhea completes a dance step with an extra flourish, arms raised to frame her face and exclaiming with delight and feeling, "Express yourself!" The cuts of Rhea's interviews and bodily movements corporeally and aesthetically make manifest "coming into her own" in the film narrative.

The variety of possessions and self-possession both material and abstract reveals a counterproject of value making within a capitalist vernacular, a counterproject over and above the "noble" work of teaching young people and financially taking care of families back home. As she asserts, "I've accepted that his reality is there and mine is here." In that moment, coming into her own is no longer living for elsewhere. Showing the Filipinas' modes of pleasure and self-making, Diaz shows not simply subjects eking out survival with some limited agency over the narrative but moments that exceed their personal narrative, beyond themselves. Instead of the image of self-negation, duty, and obligation performed by export labor, Diaz depicts forces that transform relationships around them, beyond and irreducible to their contracted labor power. After Rhea's dance sequence, Diaz immediately shows the women shopping, taking pictures of themselves, and consuming pleasure with others, the very pleasure Angel was forced to provide as a condition of her return. Instead of suffering familial indebtedness, the audience is witness to the women's delight with objects, selves, and moments of "unproductive consumption."[34] Marx defines unproductive consumption as "what the worker consumes over and above that minimum for his own pleasure," but he takes care to point out that this is from the viewpoint of capitalist ideologists. Life production lies elsewhere, particularly in the flourish of hands, arms, and voices raised. In Rhea's desire to "express herself" in her dance-cum–beauty regimen outside of teaching and family care, self making is also world making.

Like Dorothea's karaoke, Rhea's Zumba moment allows other types of embodiments and selves to emerge. Each of the women, whether in language, body, or place, take or reclaim time out of a lifetime made into a commodity and gesture bodily to another order in the world. The seemingly trivial gestures momentarily exceed tropes that reduce lifetimes and free time into labor-time, as Marx would have it in the epigraph that opens this chapter. The capacity for life making exists alongside labor-time and in tension with capitalist captures. Each performance stages and captures the seeming impossibility of generating a space outward. They index the impossibility of simple returns and the neat management of multiple

affects demanded of flexible labor. Yet they also conjure magical transformations, a karaoke song, a Disney walk, or self-help incantations during Zumba class. These are other worlds and conversations articulated
through the available vernacular of a disenchanted world that reintroduce
elements of magic and beauty in desperate circumstances. In this mode,
these impossible subjects redirect valuation and value making by taking
on another voice, time, and even body. They generate lingering impressions in their sensorial arrival, paving a path and texture to which they
exhort others to inhabit. The subject's *dating* as affect signals other possibilities for themselves and others.

In Diaz's performative cuts and the women's capture of time, various
iterations of arrival serve as disruptions to the present so that other visions
of the future emerge. I consider *dating* here to interrupt an understanding
of time as a chronology on which return or redemption depends—a sequence of events that could be recalled or be made discrete for easy
emplotment. Rather, *dating* is about bending the time and space of the
present wherein someone's appearance becomes a moment of other possibilities that was not there before the arrival. In other words, *dating* is
not just about time as duration but also about timing and the timely, or
kairos, which I will discuss in the next chapter, that intangible eventuality not wholly about individual intention but the deployment of social
conditions to configure other possibilities.

2 / "Holding Out for Something Better": Timing and Other In-Between Times

"Today the peso was 68.2 to the euro. Not a good day for mailing money home, Cely decided. She knew it was unlikely to change soon, definitely not likely to get any better, but she kept holding out anyway. That's the way she thought of it: holding out for something better."[1] Michelle Cruz Skinner's final short story in her triptych, "The Company of Strangers," begins with Cely, an undocumented Filipina domestic worker in Italy. A casual habit for the migrant worker, watching the exchange rate anticipates the opportunity to add more value to her labor, a form of speculation by speculative capital such as Cely the domestic worker. Ascribing this socialization to post-Taylorist activity, the philosopher Paolo Virno asserts that this "abstraction of opportunity" interpellates the subject into opportunism as "a game with no time-outs and no finish."[2] Perhaps this anticipation as promise and curse allows further insight into migrant chronicities. In "holding out for something better," Cely negotiates both linear time (*chronos*) and timing (*kairos*), the chronological and the timely. The first is the succession of moments, as I mentioned in the last chapter in terms of redemption and return, held together by their passing, quantified and intervalized by the workday or the calendar. The second is a chronic quality that I explore throughout this book, one that orders and signifies time's passing. "Holding out" for Cely is a distancing and tactical stance whereby she can observe conditions and decide when to intervene to shift the order (*taxis*, from which we derive "tactics") of things perhaps in her favor, perhaps not. As in all speculation, Cely dwells in this chronic in-between in the hopes that time can be made to work for her instead of the other way around.

Reading contemporary short stories by Michelle Cruz Skinner, Mia Alvar, and Nathan Go, this chapter explores the textures of inhabiting this chronic in-between, those qualitative moments of possibility against the quantification of everyday living. The contemporary short stories I treat here portray characters in various affective work and class strata—a domestic in Italy, a special education teacher in Bahrain, and a fortune-teller/ masseur across four hundred years of Philippine history—who, finding themselves on unsteady ground in their workplaces, attempt to make sense of their life trajectories within narratives of economy, so to speak.[3] Employing the short story genre, these narratives of economy invite writerly and readerly exploration within the economy of narrative time.[4] Outlining the historical comparison among literary genres, Mary Louise Pratt points to the association of the short story genre with the moment of truth or moment of insight.[5] The form's relative brevity condenses narrative time toward the emotional impact of a moment in the story. The genre in some cases allows sharp plot or emotional pivots wherein characters gain some sort of insight or, in the religious sense, experience an epiphany.

The theological and vernacular senses of epiphany are imbricated in the meaning attributed to events and their emplotment. In Christian theology, epiphany is the manifestation of the divine in the human world, "the eternal breaking into temporal."[6] This temporal breach complicates Virno's notion of the impossibility of a "time-out" in the socialization to work, in that impossibility as such occurs outside of a chronological understanding of time. In the vernacular sense, an epiphany could rupture the continuity of the characters' past, present, and future; resignify the past sequence of events and their consequences; and effectively shift the characters' place in story's world. Suggesting divine ruptures, kairotic instances underscore how time is "qualitative and experiential" and that its elements are dispersed and not altogether quantifiable.[7] In these narratives of economy, I highlight how the authors nuance this qualitative break for characters living and working at the point of their own erasure from the social world of the text. Refusing, multiplying, or gambling at that temporal break draws attention to in-between times—speculation, meantimes, and blind futurity. Complicating the texture of capital-driven temporal flows that would fix the characters' individuated identities and capacities, these timely frictions and fictions bring to light vital exchanges and value making that generate possibilities for world making and communing otherwise.

In the Company of Strangers: Speculating with Labor-Time

Skinner's short story triptych "The Company of Strangers" touches on the weak links that make up the household of Filipino domestic workers in Italy working in an unnamed ambassador's residence. As the triptych's title suggests, the protagonists, Cely, a domestic, and Sal, a gardener, are compelled by employment, formal and informal, to inhabit spaces with virtual strangers. While not necessary to their particular household function, this proximity obliges characters to make fleeting connections to place and other people as an unspoken condition of remaining employed and staying in the country. While the effort to maintain these fleeting friendships is obscured, these speculative kinships provide provisional stability and carve spaces for capacities beyond their function as gardener or domestic. The three loosely chronological but discontiguous stories reflect the characters' proximity and occasional connection with other members of a household, only to disappear into the task or into the next story.

The individual story titles of the triptych index an ever-widening world, from a flower in the garden in "Yellow Jasmine," to the expatriate household and its limits in "The Company of Strangers," and finally to global currency in "The Exchange Rate." The older but newly employed gardener, Salvador, narrates "Yellow Jasmine," which introduces the everyday rhythms of the household; Sal also narrates the second eponymous "The Company of Strangers," which stages a series of meetings between Sal and the newly fired younger domestic Cely; and finally, "The Exchange Rate" is narrated by Cely, who, since her firing, works informally as a housecleaner in private homes, including that of her new Italian boyfriend's sister-in-law. The scalar move in Skinner's title choices from the small poetic image of a jasmine flower to the vague capital flows of money reflects the types of imbricated worlds of the global and the intimate that cut through the characters' everyday lives. The flower, household, and currency as mediating conceits in each story are controlled respectively by ever smaller time frames that overlap in the protagonist's life: nature's seasonal cycle, the workday, and money's circulation. Indeed, these disparate movements require different types of attentiveness to time's passing from the characters and shape how Cely and Sal shape their relationship to places, strangers, colleagues, and new friends around them.

The final story, "The Exchange Rate," opens to find Cely noting the currency exchange rate as she rushes for buses to work, waits for bosses in order to be paid, and runs from a job interview at a clothing factory to a dinner appointment. Obsessed with clock time, "She paused to check the time in a shop on the corner then turned right, hurrying. She got to the apartment a little before nine, according to the clock sitting on the kitchen counter. Signora Antonucci looked as unhappy as usual to see her" (120). Her frenzied movement is dictated by the work day and running after potential income: "She would have to wait until the woman got back to get paid. . . . She had a three-thirty appointment for a job near her apartment. The signora should be back by two, which meant that Cely could make the appointment" (120–21). Informally employed, Cely must be the manager of her own time. Cely keeps looking at every clock on the counter or in a shop to check not only her punctuality but gauge how much time and income might have been lost: "On the bus," however, "she mused about how pleasant it was to manage her own time. . . . In spite of the smaller salary, she felt happier" (122).

In the evening, the clock-dependent narration gives way to surreptitious observations from Cely's point of view about a dinner with her boyfriend Franco and his sister-in-law Silvana, who is also one of her employers. Franco picks her up for dinner and shows her a newspaper article about illegal immigrants in Italy. Cely chooses not to tell Franco about the job interview for fear he will report her as undocumented, if ever their relationship soured: "Franco would turn her in" (123), she was sure. At the dinner, Cely is witness to gestures of affection between Silvana and Franco. Silvana is clearly cheating on her unsuspecting husband, Franco's brother. Cely gathers this information and observes all things unsaid. Her viewing point as the unrelated outsider at the table becomes valuable as one who has access to the intimacies of family life. She might later be able to use the knowledge to protect herself, his silence for hers, if Franco threatens to report her to the authorities. Every human interaction Cely has or bears witness to she assays for how it might benefit or cost her. The party pays for the dinner, and Skinner ends the story in suspended stasis: "They all sat waiting for the change" (125). When will she extricate herself from the dinner, or from Italy and away from the company of *these* strangers? When will she pull up stakes to exchange euros into pesos?

What Cely manages is the time between working and the opportunities of making more at another job. Virno describes this opportunistic frenzy as a socialized affect: "Spare time takes the form of urgency, tempestuousness, ruin: urgency for nothing, tempestuousness in being tempestuous, ruin of the self. The rapid acquiescence of the opportunist turns the imaginary struggle over the work day, over time, into an exhibition of a universal timeliness."[8] Indeed, this condition for contingent or casual labor, for those in what is now known as the faltering gig economy, is about the lack of a social safety net, but the urgency is not for nothing. For Cely, the passage of time is an opportunity for wage making and also for maximizing the value of her wages by waiting for a better currency exchange rate. Cely's quick, almost automatic, noting of the exchange rate depicts a domestic worker deploying speculative capital even while being produced as such. The practice of speculation isn't solely the domain of capitalism, after all. Rather, speculation for her spills onto other domains of unequal power in personal relationships, imagination, and uneven futures, and this informs her qualitative sense of time's passing.

Thinking through "speculative surplus," the Asian American studies critic Grace Hong looks at representations of Asian elites as mobile finance capital in popular culture. She considers how surplus acquires currency, tracing it back to Marx's notion of speculative capital:

> In Marx's terms, "fictitious capital" is what David Harvey has described as "money that is thrown into circulation as capital without any material basis in commodities or productive activity." Marx observes that fictitious capital is "never designed to be spent as capital," and indeed, Harvey notes that "interest-bearing capital [another term for speculative capital] can best fulfil its . . . functions if it preserves its flexibility in relation to specific uses, if it remains perpetually *outside of* production and *uncommitted* to specific products." In other words, speculative capital is never intended to be anything but fictitious and can do what it does best if it avoids labor or even the commodities created by labor.[9]

As Hong underscores, this ungrounded quality of speculative capital, detached from labor or commodities, keeps this capital circulating. Speculative capital derives potency from its continual promise of difference as interest profit that is "outside of production and uncommitted to specific products."[10] Therefore, money, as a representational fiction, universalizes the value of time so that commodities can be exchanged. Its value fluctuates with financial sector sentiment about national and regional economies but also in response to the unequal power between these nations and regions. What Cely notes in the exchange rate reveals the shifting value of money as itself a commodity in the global exchange.

For Cely, biding time is active stasis in between time, a habitat at which she locates and assesses the intersection of possibilities along different scales: personal, national, and global. Cely's life- and labor-time may have been exchanged for money in contracted (ongoing and future) work, but she directs how to create more value for her time. Once earned, money is her exchangeable commodity, but the variability of currency exchange itself is a constant reminder that her labor and the relationships that the remittance symbolizes take place not only within a human kinship network but simultaneously in a global financial network. Even as she tries to maximize value by waiting, the fact of currency exchange itself belies the global inequity that compelled migration in the first place, wherein global South nations and regions are transformed into sources of cheap labor whose time is in turn devalued. She dwells and dwells upon not only in-between time but in between these two places considered of unequal (read, racialized and gendered) value. In material terms, the currency conversion is crucial for both her as sender and her recipient to maximize the quantitative value as well as the qualitative meaning of distance and time away from her family. More is more, in this case. Indeed, Cely's situation is not likely to get better, but change or transformation is not necessarily about amelioration.

Cely's casual noting of the exchange rate in the beginning also serves as the literalization of the fluctuating and free-floating values of relationships between the characters at the dinner table later. As the surreptitious relationships around the table bring out, value is about who has power over whom. Cely is not only a housecleaner and girlfriend but also serves as the cover for the boyfriend's affair with his brother's wife. All the relationships at the table, not just Cely's, are speculative, each party hoping to extract some emotional or economic advantage from another now or in the future. Thus one can read the "change" they are waiting for in the end as both what is left over of the money and as that free-floating surplus, the extraneous force, that promises to alter conditions and break out of each character's stasis. The fictions projected on the amorous and familial attachments and their disavowals are what bind the group together despite mutual betrayals. What keeps them "stuck" together is the fiction that the desired object could change or deliver them from their current circumstances, but working just as powerfully alongside that are the secrets one holds over the other, knowledge that could upend another's life. Promise of a different life and threat of upheaval at once seem to dictate the terms of the erotic charge of the love quadrangle within which Cely is only incidental. Dispensable as a cleaner but indispensable as romantic cover, Cely finds a "place" in this gamble of relationships that yields temporary comfort and stability, at least until the next opportunity presents itself.

Speculative capital in the form of labor, money, relationships, and knowledge supplies an experiential and qualitative sense to time in anticipation around fantasy and futurity. The fictionality of fictitious capital is what leads Cely and the other characters to inhabit both the possibility of change and material dead ends at once. In *The Filipino Primitive*, Sarita See revisits speculation in Carlos Bulosan's short story "Magno Rubio."[11] Rather than seeing spendthrift practices and bad gambles of the impoverished agricultural workers as wasteful and counterproductive, See argues that such wastefulness is intentional speculation on the part of the illiterate, who envisions the future not necessarily as one of progressive improvement but in terms of leaps and bounds beyond their current situation. Yet the desire to conjure a future in leaps and bounds refuses the inevitability and denies the purported fairness of the unequal situation. Furthermore, the desire signals skepticism toward the promise of amelioration on terms dictated by those who wield power. Time as currency could be wasted unproductively and gambled away on bad bets. Wasting time or money in seemingly unproductive ways steals time and denies its potential value, appropriating it for one's own world-making capacity.

Similarly, Cely biding time with her new friends deploys time for her own gamble, rather than surrendering to its inevitability as determined by her relationship to her boyfriend or the Italian state. Holding out for something better, whether in currency exchange or life circumstances, is tactical deferral to exact the optimal terms of exchange when the subject has little choice. In the same way that Cely creates more value for her wages by simply waiting, she accumulates and defers sharing knowledge, in hopes that it will have more value later, a form of speculation. What appears in the final scene as nonaction or stasis is a tactical use, or ordering, of time. The deferral of exchange hopes to ensure that it follows the proper order to imbue the act of exchange with value. As Pierre Bourdieu reminds us, the "work of time," or, more specifically, its deferral, is crucial in the ritual of gift exchange.[12] One cannot immediately give a gift in exchange, much less give the same gift in return. Time must work to mark the occasion of the initial gift, and exchange can happen only at the opportune moment. The act of qualitative assessment of the chronological makes possible the value and meaning of the act(s) and the relationship.

The final tableau is from Cely's point of view: "Cowards all of them, Cely thought bitterly" (125). Ending the narrative with this tableau, Skinner plays with seeming stasis and the potential disruption simmering beneath that could eventually destroy the patina of harmony among the love quadrangle. The story will end when, with a single eruption from any one of the characters, everything goes awry anywhere and everywhere.

The story can also go nowhere, just continue as it has, with simmering resentment from those at the table. As Cely describes to Franco her relationship with the sister-in-law for whom she cleans, the underlying tensions generate smaller bursts of violence: "She speaks as if she wants to yell. As if inside she's thinking evil thoughts about me" (121). In either case, the suspended moment is a turbulent one. "Suspension as both a spatial and temporal category," as Gopinath asserts in the context of queer diasporic aesthetics and belonging, "may allow for a momentary vantage point from which to envision an alternative to the here and now."[13] This tableau moment is as close as Skinner allows Cely to her moment of insight, the point where she accumulates information. She takes in the various nuances, secrets, pretenses, pressure points, and weak spots of the relationships around the table. As Kathleen Stewart observes of what might seem like an innocuous scene, the tableau is "an ordinary saturated with affect's lines of promise and threat."[14] The characters all sit waiting, the moment sedimented with secrets and emotions just under the surface that could turn sour or joyous at any minute. Through observation and reflection, Cely takes in the affective lines at the table to think about her future and to assess the right time to remove herself from relationships, use information, or exchange money. Cely's affective mode puts pressure on what in the first half of the story would indicate only a desire to convert time into money. Speculative kinship here leaves open the possibilities of extracting value from others, not necessarily monetary value, but to meet other needs in her life, including company, care, direction for the future, and conditions for exodus.

By contrast, in "Yellow Jasmine" and "The Company of Strangers" Skinner explores speculative kinships not necessarily about extracting advantage from other people but about expanding into a sensory world and into past lives. On Sal's first day in Italy in the household, "he had to trim the bushes in the garden" (93). Skinner continues, "He'd just finished a breakfast of rice and fish and coffee, which had seemed strange to him in such a faraway place" (93). He was in the company of strangers despite the household staff's shared Filipino origins. The narration is quiet and usually informed by Sal's impressions about people and place, which build up with each encounter. The passage is illustrative of how Skinner narrates Sal's point of view with a doubled sense of time and position. There is temporal tension between the anxious anticipatory "he had to" in the first sentence, followed by a past-perfect narration, "he'd just finished," rather than simply "finished," in the next. The older character's interior and exterior, future and past play off each other as if each event is already informed by a previous event or has occurred any number of other times.

Though bound to others by the work cycle, as Cely was, Sal experiences the household through mechanisms not measurable by clock time. For Sal, place and belonging gradually emerge as affective accretions. That is, the household is not so much a pregiven world but one that is slowly built as Sal forms a sensory relationship to each place and person. This sedimentation of time and affect is most pointed when it comes to his primary object of care, the garden:

> When he'd arrived last night, he paused only briefly in his room to leave his suitcase. Then, he'd stepped out into the garden that would now be *his* to care for. First, he'd closed his eyes and smelled. Each garden had a smell. This one smelled of an almost-familiar sweet flower. He had also smelled grass and earth and other plants he couldn't identify. He had looked around and seen a dark patch between some trees. The vegetable garden the cook was showing him this morning.
>
> (95–96)

Sal reads his surroundings through sight, smell, and taste. It is through the sensorial that he eventually expresses ownership. By alternating between Sal's first impressions of events and their subsequent daily iterations, the reader is witness to Sal's efforts to make things smooth for the household. The narrative style thus depicts how Sal's observations begin to populate the household with other characters, expanding his world from the garden to other people. Connecting him to others is the work schedule. The invitation of Ben, the cook, to eat initiates him to the daily routine: "'Lunch is at 12:30,' said Ben. 'But I usually put out some merienda at 10'" (93–94). The driver, cook, gardener, nursemaid, and two maids under one household are connected by moments that are nonproductive: breaks, lunches, weekends, and days off. As he learns the ways of the household, his encounters with other members and with the garden in particular shape his relationship with place by way of other and past places: "Sal smelled the jasmine and thought of home" (108).

Aside from his sensorial capacities, Sal keeps wondering about the previous gardener, his predecessor's organization of the tools, ability to speak and read Italian, why he left (96, 98). All are questions about continuity. After all, Sal is dealing with living things, sentient and not, which continue to thrive even in the absence of any gardener. His task is to recognize the signs of past work so he might continue it seamlessly: "The line of the previous trim was still visible" because "it was meant to be a circular shape, he could tell, but he had to keep checking that it wasn't too wide or too flat" (96, 99). In one sense, he must continually converse with both the garden and his absent predecessor. His predecessor's choices live in this ecology, and Sal's intimate knowledge of gardening, his craft, makes possible the call and response with the previous gardener. Sal's shaping of environment, including the grounds and garden that sustain the household, is his household duty. However, the grounds and garden cease to be simply inanimate objects produced by a gardener; rather, for Sal, contained in his capacities is a continuous sensing of activity, life, and aesthetic choices made by another on a living system.

While the household rhythm provides daily continuity and repetition, the effort of getting along with others is an intentional activity beyond his function as a gardener. Fitting into the household as a process entails comprehending the environment, the garden, and the household as an intricate ecology of sensation and meanings. To become part of the rhythm of the work day is to become part of the ecology of strangers, including living and nonliving objects, the garden, and the workers that have come before him. His marking time with others in a shared space is a form of communal acknowledgment as a working *member* of a household. It is not an assemblage of machinic parts, after all, but the embodiment of seamless linking to others' rhythm of movement and the ability to create continuity across time and bodies.

Continuity and activity also signify something else for Sal, beyond the employer's needs or for the smooth working of the household, as he continues his story in "The Company of Strangers." Sal's desire to continue another person's work as well as his visits to the newly fired Cely also make up for a lost connection. He had once hoped that his recently deceased nephew would continue his vocation: "He didn't tell Miche [the driver] about his sister's eldest who had died last year. Sal had been training the boy to work with him and had secured him a job as an assistant" (103–4).

> Sal paused in his picking of the potato leaves and sighed. He wiped his eyes. He knew his sadness over Ninoy would pass as had so many other sadnesses, fading with time. He wiped his eyes and nose with the back of his hand, sniffled. After a few deep breaths, he went back to his work, plucking each leaf carefully, with a bit of stem. Ben had said he would put them in a soup tomorrow. Sal thought that would make him feel better.
>
> (117)

His careful tending of his patch of soil is not only his stake in belonging but one that contains and tends his private grief. The narration suggests an unintentional exchange of care between Ben and Sal: Sal grows the familiar leaf to be served in a soup the next day. The exchange will pass unnoticed as part of the daily ritual among staff. While unintended, the affective significance will remain unarticulated but articulated and effected just the same. One can thus read the moment of truth when he wipes away a tear, remembering his dead nephew, as a recognition of continuity and replacement that is rendered impossible for Sal. Yet that substitution yields something more. Denied filiative continuity, Sal is left with life-knowledge to be passed on through affinity, aesthetics, and sustenance into the garden and the household. This knowledge is significant in material and abstract terms for himself and his fellow staff through communal but undetectable and invaluable reciprocity.

In this quiet triptych of stories where nothing quite happens, Skinner points to the tensions within kairotic time. In classical rhetoric, *kairos* suggests that a speech act, in order to be effective, must be appropriate to the occasion, so as not to disturb the social order. For example, a toast or eulogy must hit the correct tone of celebration or mourning. Another perspective on timeliness in direct tension with this idea foregrounds the speaker or actor's ability to *make* the moment apposite through the speech or act itself. The tension between these notions of timeliness is the line between social rules and individual improvisation within the bounds of those rules. Does one follow or break the social rhythm to shift surroundings? This familiar tension is that between sameness or difference cutting through time. To have the desired effect on the audience, the act ought to follow expectations, that is, convention and decorum, or if not, one must improvise to make it seem apposite in the moment. To be apposite, from the Latin *ad ponere*, to place toward, implies a positioning toward or a placement in relationship or proximity to another.[15] Paradoxically, the apposite disrupts and disappears at the same time. The appositional phrase in a sentence, for example, brackets itself off by commas. The phrase's placement in the sentence marks it as wholly extraneous, yet it immutably shifts and redirects in varying degrees the meaning of the whole thought. The apposition disrupts the flow of the sentence to signal but not insist on its relevance.

Migrant lives are often lived in apposition rather than straightforward opposition as they develop speculative kinships that generate affective connections however weak or dispersed. How to negotiate that compelled proximity is the issue for both Cely and Sal. For Cely to live in Italy as a domestic, given her undocumented status, is to be on continual, though not constant, watch for speculative opportunities to leverage relationships. For Sal, in a patch of soil on foreign ground, these speculative links in apposition yield sensory and affective meanings to define his place in and alongside his function as a gardener. Both live in apposition to colleagues, friends, houses (not their own), and countries (not or no longer their own). To act in apposition, therefore, requires a tactical positioning and subtle directional shift in a situation. Tactic is placement and arrangement (taxis). Better yet, as the minor chord to strategy, it is improvisational ordering that shifts even momentarily a larger complex of conditions. Here I echo Moten and Harney's use of the word to refer to fugitives in other institutions, an "appositionality" of "being together in homelessness. . . . Not simply to be among his own; but to be among his own in dispossession, to be among the ones who cannot own, the ones who have nothing and who, in having nothing, have everything."[16] Speculative kinship involves the creative capacity to take time and space and redirect these ever so slightly, almost seamlessly, so as not to disturb the fictional sheen of the surface. However, smooth surfaces could as easily conceal turbulence elsewhere.

The Miracle Worker: Proliferating Meantimes

Mia Alvar's short story "The Miracle Worker," in her collection *In the Country*, centers on a young, middle-class Filipina special education teacher, Sally Rivas, an "oil wife" to a Filipino engineer working in Bahrain. The story deals with segregated, interclass relations. Characters, gestures, and objects circulate in obscured registers, indicating radically different significance along the segregated racial and class strata of Bahraini-Filipino society. Sally's friend Minnie, a domestic helper, introduces Sally to her employer Mrs. Mansour to help with her disabled daughter, Aroush. Mrs. Mansour feels ostracized from her Bahraini circles because of her learning-disabled daughter, deemed by her family to be a consequence of an improper marriage match. At the end of the short story, Sally realizes that the work she is expected to do for Mrs. Mansour has nothing to do with her professional training as a teacher but is instead to uphold the fantasy that her training is bestowing progress and normalization on the child.

After weeks of lying about the cognitive progress of her student, Sally decides to invite her employer to her home to discuss with her the limits of Sally's expertise and the child's abilities. As Sally begins to explain Aroush's severe limitations, Mrs. Mansour immediately interrupts:

> "Thank you again for bringing us to this place . . . It is like Paradise."
> A kind of paradise was what she paid me for, after all: the dream of Aroush's bright future. She replaced the sunglasses atop her cheekbones, a warning I understood; whatever I wish to illuminate, she

was happy in the dark. What I had thought of as deception was my duty. If I cared to keep Aroush in my life, *this* was the service I had to keep providing, whether or not I thought better of it. And so I held my tongue and treaded water, looking up at where Mrs. Mansour's eyes were hidden from me. From a distance perfect strangers would assume that Mrs. Mansour was my *amo*, and I a servant at her feet.[17]

The scene takes place in the privacy of Sally's house, now transformed into the employer's "paradise," a fantasy time and place segregated and hidden away from her upper-class Bahraini peers. When Sally tries to bring up the reality of Aroush's and her own teacherly limitations, Mrs. Mansour's expression of heartfelt gratitude becomes instead a stern warning from an employer. Supplicant becomes adversary in that instant. For Mrs. Mansour, the daughter's disability is no longer about karmic cruelty but now the result of professional incompetence. For Sally, the warning takes away the foundations of Sally's authority as childhood education expert, revealing how she is simply another temporary service worker treading water in a hidden desert paradise. Alvar ends the short story with this mise-en-scène: The narrator precariously treads water, supporting the child, as the mistress suns herself on a lounge by the pool. The ending is remarkable: Sally realizes that, as part of her informally remunerated service, one of the miracles she is meant to perform is to make herself and Aroush disappear into the world of her making.

In the meantime, within the short story are stories not quite like Sally's and also rendered invisible to her because of her class position. That is, Sally's invisibility by design is only one of the many types of occlusions in class-stratified Bahraini society, even among Filipino workers. If social worlds coexist invisible to one another in the short story, to focus on one "moment of truth," such as the ending, casts aside or subordinates other, seemingly inconsequential elements of plot. I use "inconsequential" here to mean both that which seems unimportant to the plot but also that which evades consequence. The moment of truth and the inconsequential both mark discontinuities in the text. Looking beyond the ending for the moment of truth, I note that Alvar includes and leaves unresolved two disturbing events that cannot be readily integrated into the compressed plot. The domestic and service workers' strike happening outside the house does not end on its own terms. A young, newly arrived Filipina domestic commits suicide, which effectively ends the strike with no resolution. Later, Sally discovers that her beloved student has been abused by her longtime friend, Minnie. The poolside realization of her social place opens to other worlds as hidden in the story as her own.

Capital relations engineer these occlusions, which are made possible by the class stratification that creates distinct social worlds. This suggests a simultaneity of events, meantimes, wherein the meanings of the same gestures and objects change in each context. What I call "meantimes" suggest other places and stories that share elements but do not necessarily partake in the same system of meanings. These meantimes are made apparent not because of an alternative mode of production but in considering other modes of exchange that generate other uses of time and objects. Tracing the circulation of gifts and gestures reveals connected multiple social worlds rendered invisible to one another, much as Mrs. Mansour's paradise is to Sally and Bahraini society.

The work of proximity shapes relations and environments for those cared for, to be sure, but capital relations enable the occlusion of labor, identities, and spaces from one another such that the simultaneity of times appears as miracles, as the title suggests. Those who practice the healing arts—health, teaching, and care professionals—are sometimes called miracle workers, seeming to accomplish extrahuman feats, suggesting the calling forth of the divine to intervene in human affairs, bodies, and spaces.[18] Sally's job was to bring Mrs. Mansour and Aroush to "this place . . . like Paradise." The efficacy of Sally's labor as a teacher is evidenced by the transformation of environment, atmosphere, and relationships for Aroush and Mrs. Mansour, but most important for Mrs. Mansour is how Sally's middle-class home keeps Aroush hidden from the close-knit Bahraini community. Applied to service labor, whether teacher or caregiver, the alleged miracle is achieved by disarticulating the human labor necessary from the socioeconomic design in capital relations that makes the fantasy of progress and social harmony imaginable. Temporal discontinuity figured in the notion of the thaumatological is therefore an effect of fantasy around affective work and not of the divine.

With her husband, Sally is valued by the states of the Philippines and Bahrain not only as mobile labor, but based on their heterosexual and class identities, they are able to cultivate and occupy a parallel private domestic space in the host society.[19] As an "oil wife," Sally's marital status provides domestic respectability to her husband's middle-management position. Sally's paid but informal employment with Mrs. Mansour and Aroush takes advantage of the incidental terms outside of Sally's husband's official contract with an oil company in Bahrain. That is, since the husband has the official contract, Sally's status as oil wife makes her a surplus figure and also potential informal speculative labor in the host country. The labor Sally represents—her time, her education, gender, sexuality, class, race, and home—activates its potential value once she meets

Mrs. Mansour. Sally's advanced degree in special education allows her to enter the social field not as a domestic servant, like her friend Minnie, but as a respectable bourgeois subject like Mrs. Mansour. However, her ethnoracial identity segregates her domestic space from those of the elite Bahraini community. Sally's work of proximity demands labor of similitude, to be *like* Mrs. Mansour, but subordinate, to create for her something *like* Paradise, because it is hidden.

Sally's unaccounted time and domestic space is racialized and given differential value *even before* the extraction of her labor-time with Mrs. Mansour. In this informal economy, the qualitative value and play of sameness and difference between the two women founded upon gender, race, sexual, and class hierarchies make the teacher-student relationship valuable for her informal employer. Mrs. Mansour first enters Sally's home with great secrecy: "Once the outer gate had shut, she parted her jilbab to reveal a gold-embroidered bodice and a little daughter. 'Here is Aroush,' said Mrs. Mansour. The child had been anchored on her hip and concealed by her clothes all along" (28). Adjacent but not inside a Bahraini household like a domestic worker, Sally remains invisible and outside the Bahraini world. The divine paradise as staged by Sally has value for Mrs. Mansour precisely because it is obscured. Sally's ability to occupy middle-class privacy as an oil wife, literalized by "the house," extends Mrs. Mansour's cloak that hides Aroush from view. The way gender and class similitude covers over racial difference is critical to capital's ability to extract surplus value in social reproduction. As David Roediger has observed, race management is not only about competition among "races" but also a series of proxies and substitutions to effect the smooth workings of social reproduction, that which effects Sally's disappearance.[20] What seemed like an opportunity to practice her profession is actually by design a process of disarticulations between service and servitude so that she may absorb and render invisible Mrs. Mansour's daughter with her own invisibility. Like her engineer husband, who acts as the managerial buffer between Indian subordinates and Arab bosses, Sally, hidden away within the trappings of a middle-class house, serves to cloak her employer's social and domestic imperfections by serving as temporary mother-substitute in the guise of a teacher.

Mrs. Mansour buys Sally's time through wages but also through her trust and affections. She continually gives her small but extravagant gifts, "a diamond-encrusted tie clip" or "a box of golf-tees made of eighteen-karat gold" (46). As gratuities, these gifts stand in for the unquantifiable "extra" service of care Sally provides for Aroush and Mrs. Mansour. "Time and money sold separately" (46), Sally's husband mockingly quips of the over-the-top but ultimately useless objects. Sally's time and Mrs. Mansour's money are indeed commodities circulated to buy Mrs. Mansour intangibles such as fantasy (progress for her daughter) and emotions (affection). Finding no use for the gifts, Sally gives Minnie these luxurious objects. Sally rationalizes regifting the objects as an act of resistance or even as a redistribution of wealth. Between Mrs. Mansour and Sally and between Sally and Minnie, the gift exchange signifies at once differing class positions and the desire to erase those lines in the illusion of family gifting. Minnie in turn passes the gifts on to relatives in Manila or uses them as prizes at local church raffles. The chain of redistribution would provide the material links down the global class hierarchy. The tie clip or other expensive item is recirculated downward and outward to a proliferation and chain of "minor minor characters," as Marte-Wood has termed them.[21] The ever-diminishing representation of characters and events registers the ever-diminishing representability of identities (or identities made unrepresentable) because they do not partake in the original capitalist mode of exchange, though the gift may originate from that very exchange. The resignification of the exchange outside these alters and reveals other operations in the exchange. Focusing on the object as act of resistance or compliance to capitalist relations renders invisible other worlds in the various downward exchanges beyond Mrs. Mansour's or Sally's control. The object's recirculation escapes this binary altogether, as it takes on other meanings outside either.

While Sally's "extra" time has been quantified and paid for by these objects, the downward circulation of gifts suggests other social worlds happening in the meantime and other values generated apart from labor-time as value. What other qualitative life processes does regifting make possible? While gifts represent the "extra" element that binds and bonds giver and recipient, the acts of giving or regifting engroups in various and unpredictable ways, and each instance nuances the relationship between value and vital life-making worlds. The tie clip, for example, signified a luxury item given as a token of friendship and exchange between Mrs. Mansour and Sally for time and labor. Alluded to but not part of the story's frame is the circulation of the objects as a raffle in some Filipino gathering. In the context of a church or community raffle, the prize is secondary to the process whereby the community is constituted by joining the activity and the (often exaggerated) reactions to who wins. The raffle as event is a form of collective gambling that allows members to put in small stakes to win a bigger prize. The objects as prizes are not as important as the process of joining, the suspense of picking a winner, and the joy and adulation of seeing who the winner is. These are the vital points of gathering or engroupment made possible by the raffle as activity, not the object, which is only incidental to it.

In another instance, the human smile is the gesture that appears, is exchanged, and comes to have different meanings in the story. Minnie and her fellow domestic workers had gone on strike, and "the union had floated other, subtler strategies. Withholding smiles, for one. It had worked for the cashiers in Italy, omitting personal gestures that appeared nowhere in their job descriptions but nonetheless brought management to its knees" (44). In the strikers' case, the smile as human action is a commodity that is expected of service workers. When withheld as part of the service, it had succeeded in Italy as a strike tactic. The transaction or specified work was accomplished, but withholding the smile refuses the human connection accompanying the money exchange. Though only incidental to the service, the qualitative human connection has become an expected and intrinsic part of purchasing a commodity, part of customer satisfaction; it signals surplus compliance while at the same time erasing traces of labor and effort. The smile is the surplus human, though unnecessary, touch to money exchange but becomes part of the experiential life of the transaction and commodity.

In the story's structure, Aroush's smile resonates with the smile withheld by the domestic workers as part of their work stoppage, which inspires Sally's mini-rebellion against Mrs. Mansour. In one of her sessions with Aroush, Sally glances over at her student to see "a smile. It went away, but I had seen it. I felt as shocked as if she'd spoken a full sentence or stood and walked around the room. It was the closest thing to a miracle I had ever witnessed, and I'd done nothing to cause or earn it" (47). She takes Aroush's smile as a gift. Unlike Mrs. Mansour's gifts, Aroush's smile represents for Sally not a transaction but a communicative connection across two beings with differing capacities for pain and pleasure. To report the smile to her employer would have reduced the gesture to a sign of the child's progress and a result expected of Sally's productivity. By withholding the information, she cuts the child's gesture from its other use as product, a deliverable issuing from her professional expertise. Preserving the smile as a miracle for herself enables a private fantasy as a parental figure, a life that she intentionally did not choose for herself and her husband. For Sally, Aroush's smile opens a distinct world away from the desert paradise, away from the husband's oilfield, away from other Filipino workers, a place and moment only she and Aroush inhabit. Not added value as with the clerk, the same gesture emerging from remunerated affective work is a reminder that affective work is a complex trans-subjective activity that creates more than its intended effects.

The terms of affective exchange, rather than the objects involved in the exchange, unsettle the various meanings of exchange that do not align with seamless narratives around capital's flow or labor's resistance to this flow. Rather than focus on the origin, destination, or agents of exchange, I underscore the import of looking at the various modes of exchange along the chain to reveal the qualitative character of life activities, the nonvaluable surplus that capital often seeks to harness. This attention is critical when the chain of exchange involves qualitative "services of proximity," both paid and unpaid, that delineate multiple relationships all at once. Focusing on the objects exchanged might obscure relationality present in any proffering. That is, the character, action, and object can take on different meanings according to the social world in which the exchange occurs, whether given, shared, offered, bought, found, bartered, or gifted between people. Veering away from the conundrum of objects and agents as separate entities, attention to flows in between times of exchange make palpable the texture of labor-time and life-times. The proffering creates other relationships, spaces, and times of habitation even within a network of national, racial, classed, and gendered hierarchies.

Doubt is cast on Sally's connection with Minnie, whether in community as a fictive mother or in solidarity as a fellow worker, when Sally discovers Minnie's abusive behavior toward Aroush. Both substitute child and mother, the members of her fictive kin and mechanisms for her survival, reveal other identities relationships and worlds apart from hers, and neither were ever in her control or visual range. One particularly hot day, Sally playfully splashes water on Aroush's face, and Aroush falls into a screaming fit. Wondering why Aroush had such a violent reaction to a spray of water, Sally later realizes with her professional eye that Minnie, as a domestic helper in Mrs. Mansour's home, has been torturing Aroush with a spray bottle. Sally conjectures: "I had under estimated her: what looked like a lifetime of toil and taking orders contains subversions no one, until now had seen. She'd been silently striking all along; she didn't need my protection. What arrogance, to think I should take up her cause, even the score. I was no smarter than a child, we didn't understand nuances. She was not my mother" (59). Minnie is not her mother, and neither does Minnie need her patronage; this erstwhile friendship was solely a world of her making. What fictions render visible can also obscure other capacities, identities, and events elsewhere, as with Mrs. Mansour at the poolside.

While Sally's story explores the conditions of a racialized buffer class in Bahrain as a socially necessary condition generating informal economies that define and sustain the class system, hers also complicates questions about fantasies around affective kinship. While Minnie cares for Mrs. Mansour's home, she would often spend her days off at Sally's house doing light cleaning or cooking. Separated by class, occupation, and generation, Sally nonetheless feels an affinity for Minnie, projecting a mother-daughter kinship. "Meeting Minnie felt like a reunion in some dream where my own mother thought she recognized me, then didn't" (34). In truth, only Sally can have the privilege of a family fantasy with Minnie, who cannot presume equality and such familiarity. At their very first meeting in the market, Minnie mistakes Sally for another domestic helper and becomes profusely apologetic when she finds out Sally is a professional: "She retreated so quickly from small talk to bows and helpless apologies" (34). The retreat marked their class positions despite Minnie's age seniority over Sally. For Minnie, as less educated and lower in the labor hierarchy, her cleaning and cooking become gift offerings to Sally but also condition their friendship across the class divide. The same activity has different valences in terms of their class-inflected friendship and sense of community, each occupying different terms of unfreedoms vis-à-vis employers and the host country. For Sally, she feels Minnie's care as if it were a mother caring for her daughter.

"Care" in carework is not simply a warm sentiment and a possible redemptive mode of exchange, a precursor to progress or resistance. Instead, care in the short story is posed as a challenge, whether cast as a commodity for which Sally is hired, or Minnie as substitute mother for Sally, or Aroush as student and substitute child. Commodified categories, like mother, domestic, caregiver, and teacher, render some capacities visible while obscuring others. While Sally and Minnie share some conditions of alienated labor, easy alliances in terms of cultural filiality do not necessarily produce knowledge or "care" as a mode of alternative exchange. The exchanges can also bring out the contradictions of different capacities, destructive and creative, that occupations and identities permit. Similarly, resistance is not just about the power of withholding smiles but includes the possibility of inflicting pain and fear upon a disabled child. The strike is not just the spectacle of one; it may include obscured acts coded as abuse and criminality. Resistance itself could fall under the category of abuse and crime. Sally disappears with her husband but reappears with Mrs. Mansour, who in turn makes her disappear further as a servant; Sally also becomes a fictive mother to Aroush, and Minnie a fictive mother to her—but one who then harms her beloved student. Bodies disappear and reappear in other forms. The chain of care is continually disarticulated as familiar categories—mother, employer, servant, carer—and their presumed alignment are cast asunder.

Returning to the unresolved side plots, the discovery of abuse and the newcomer's suicide insist on the narrative's own incompleteness and inexplicability, rendering Sally's main story line equally incomplete. Sally goes to the memorial service in a local classroom for the young female domestic. The other workers have come together to pitch in for a makeshift memorial and to send her body home. While listening to eulogies from other workers who barely knew the deceased, Sally thinks: *"Will I die alone, with no one to mourn me but a bunch of strangers in the classroom? Will anybody even remember who I was?"* (58). The price of alienation and loneliness could not be resolved by the kind of easy community Sally had forged with Minnie. The young woman's suicide is an instance whereby fellowship cannot provide a lifeline. The young woman decided to end her life and disrupt production altogether—all without explanation. Her death also disrupts the workers' countertime, making apparent the stark disposability of each worker's life. Their disposability, after all, is the condition of their desirability as workers. In this case, the makeshift community was not able to save a life, and the abject nature of her funeral exposes human disposability so profoundly that even the memory of her life might not register after the funeral, as Sally fears.

Rather than death and ending, concurrent events in the meantime in the story make way for plural moments of truth that signal the unfinished or the insights yet to come. The suicide, the failed strike, the invisible abuse, set off as subplots in the narrative, refuse to disappear but animate other trajectories of migrant life and death. These shadow moments are incommensurable and refuse alignment either with capital synchronicity or to narratives of resistance. Reading the short stories solely along these two lenses elides, obscures, and subordinates other messy and turbulent modes of meaning making, relating, and valuating trans-subjective worlds. Much like the short story form itself, life-activity is fragmentary, polysemic, and multidirectional. The "moment of truth" in "The Miracle Worker," when protagonist and reader tread water, forces both to reframe the events in the past and to rethink the unfolding of the future. But given the open-ended violence that Alvar includes in the story, miracles are perhaps not about grace or the divine after all but about creating the conditions for the invisible, the untouched, and the worthless to highlight the mired sedimentation of our present.

"The Blind Oracle of Mactan": Touch as a Blind Gamble

In "The Blind Oracle of Mactan," the writer Nathan Go provides a de-lightful figure for the future: a blind, impotent masseur who is also an avid gambler.[22] Proving for centuries that the future is indeed a blind gamble, the ageless oracle "has been twenty-one for 496 years," having warned Magellan of his demise in 1521, MacArthur of his failure in 1941, and the Marcoses in 1983. Now he awaits his own death. He reaches ma-turity and goes blind at twenty-one, during his encounter with Magel-lan. Go depicts the unnamed oracle-masseur as a restless youth who currently works at the Unchained Melody Massage Parlor. After centu-ries of "noodling bodies," he has bulging muscles but "sadly, he can never get it up." Having foreseen countless deaths in people's bodies through the centuries has rendered him impotent. Frozen at the peak of his at-tractiveness and youthful adulthood, he is a favorite of the ladies and "some gentlemen's too." Specializing in foot rubs, he stimulates organs through the foot's pressure points: His clients can opt for a "massage-prophecy combination."

In Go's poetic and humorous account, knowledge of the future is se-ductive and beautiful, preternaturally in the flower of youth yet impotent. The oracle "does not give out happy endings. Neither adult nor the fairy tale kind." Go plays on the reputation of massage parlors as places of sex work along with a host of other remunerated intimacies. All his clients, not surprisingly, seem to be ill-fated. He only gives bad news of the oc-casional maiming or other misfortunes. As Go cleverly puts it, the ora-cle's prophecies and body massages seem to work toward opposing ends, physical well-being bundled with psychically damaging news, leaving no one satisfied. While the oracle-masseur can manipulate the body into health, he cannot necessarily do the same for the future. Bodies are in-terwoven with their fates.

The young man's special vision, however, can also be blinded by love. He forms an attachment with a Chinese businesswoman who initially came to him for a foot rub and became a regular. While in bed together, she mentions her husband and children and an upcoming trip, so he pro-ceeds to give her a foot massage. He eagerly shares a vision with her. He sees her with the spouse and children at the successful launch of their boat. Despite the augury of good fortune, she later dies on that same boat. Despondent, he questions God about receiving a false vision. God re-sponds, "I did not send you a false prophecy. . . . You were in love." After the heartbreaking loss, the young man receives a premonition of his own death. He welcomes this news. From then on he awaits every December by the beach for the sea to take him.

Moving away from simply consuming endings as a literary transaction, the oracle's abilities may be read as more vast than providing bad endings. By touching bodies, the blind oracle touches lives to feel out their possibilities, incapacities, and failures. Like the future, the touch is erotic; contact with the foot stimulates various organs to grow or expand. In foretelling the future, the oracle-masseur presages but also enacts the kairotic, the disruption of divine time into the chronological. As he smoothes out muscular knots, he divines the body's temporal unfolding. His touch is not just manipulating bodies into vigor but also about reading the life in them. The body reveals itself to him, and he feels the body's capacities in time. For the client, knowing the future is seductive but also transactional. The oracle stimulates the body, then feels for its eventual decline or demise. Death as a "bad" fortune is a perspective the oracle's clients might have, since what is often projected as a "good" future is an able-bodied version of oneself. Anything short of that seems like a misfortune. Blind to present circumstances and only feeling the body for its promise, the oracle himself cannot derail what he sees as inevitable. What he receives is a vision, and how the client lives her life depends on how much stock she puts in the story. Prophecies as vision condition the feel of how life is lived. But what the monetary transaction does is reduce the future to one ending. After all, death is everyone's ending, excepting the oracle himself.

By the end of the short story, the ever-youthful oracle seems to have lost the will to live. Go then switches from third-person narration and turns to the audience in direct address, using an inclusive we: "And if we care for him at all, we should give him his happy ending." Perhaps he lives only for that moment of his own release: "It is a little dramatic, honestly, wishing to be drowned, even for a blind oracle. But it is the only thing he has ever wanted." While leaving the reader in suspense, Go entreats the reader to allow the oracle his death as multiple types of release: in the erotic sense, as the end of life, and as narrative closure. The author stages a reversal here that shifts the service of care work and ending to the reader. However, why *should* the reader provide this happy ending? Why might a reader feel indebted to the oracle? Why must the reader *owe* the oracle a happy ending at all?

In playfully refusing the climax to the story, the author withholds. Go violates the contract between reader and writer to provide a beginning, a middle, and an end. But he also invites the reader to intervene. Stepping aside, he appeals not necessarily to the reader's frustration; neither is he necessarily teasing to exact more from the reader. All such elements of erotic play are in play. He appeals to the reader's sympathy and implores the reader to imagine and lead the oracle's life to a satisfactory and satisfying ending for both reader and character. Or not. He tasks the reader to choose to kill the protagonist or leave him in agony for eternity. What begins as a delightful, even salacious, tale transforms suddenly into an awful vision of erotics and death. Might a vision of a future, even of death, be conjured out of pity, or even love?

For the heartbroken oracle, love strangely short-circuits the narrative lines that proscribe inevitability as well as the oracle's ability to be a divine conduit. This incapacity brought on by the love attachment may be read as another ability activated only in communion with another. What love and being with a beloved conjure is a different vision of the future. If touch links bodies together, then what he envisioned in the businesswoman was an instance of joy in and through the beloved figure. Being together enables an imagining of a possibility of another world that breaks the seeming inevitability of a single future. The vision is achieved only beside, in proximity, and only in attachment to another. In that moment of engagement with his beloved, he becomes the conduit with and for another imagining being. Perhaps he is the person beside her in the vision. Perhaps the vision of the future is simply his wish for the woman. In that exchange, his nonappearance in the vision does not denote his absence but a making manifest of the trans-subjective workings between the oracle and the beloved. The connection thus conjures a different vision, one not limited by what is proffered by the divine. At the author's supplication, the reader is asked to take the place of the oracle that must feel bodies and lives to its ending. Like the oracle and his lost beloved, together reader, writer, and character imagine this other vision not of a future but a possibility. As the oracle's plaint against God reminds him, just because a vision has not or does not come to pass does not make it false. Rather than a purchase on some inevitable ending, the gathering of imagination cultivates a sense of *kairos*, the refusal of the natural order in the everyday and the refusal of inevitability itself.

Go thus asks the reader to consider such a gamble on the oracle's waiting game. The oracle's speculative vocation and speculative habit get him into trouble and are why he is always on the move to avoid creditors and angry clients. As one of his flaws, "he loves gambling, as all oracles do." The story's reversal makes visible the affective gap between reader and character. The gap asks what imaginary worlds we can generate toward its fulfillment not in arithmetical, consumptive exchange but in relational terms. Debt is a promise made today, projected and repaid into a future that might never come. To take out debt supposes that the present is not enough and recognizes that the future is always a gamble. See suggests framing such gambles through "other modes of debt and obligation" issuing from an indigenous notion of *utang na loob* (internal, relational debt) and *kapwa* (a sense of fellow-feeling and interconnectedness)—where reciprocity, mutuality, and obligation would displace capitalist hierarchization.[23] Across alternative modes of indebtedness and value making, life making and making time work alongside capital relations. Debt without accumulation creates other effects, such as communal belonging and mutual responsibility of well-being. Even beyond such seeming altruism, such bonds acknowledge one's place born from being with another.

Across these narratives, touch across persons in the work of proximity anticipates and redirects bodies and relationships but is also by necessity an intimate and interpretive activity. Even when reduced to a commodity, knowledge of the future is a blind gamble, but the gamble itself refuses inevitability. The next chapter looks at how workers navigate the future as blind gamble when competing visions of the future are tied to global corporations and nation-state fantasies.

3 / "I Understand Where You're Coming From": Temporal Migration and Offshore Chronographies

Marketing has become the center or the "soul" of the corporation. We are taught that corporations have a soul, which is the most terrifying news in the world.

—GILLES DELEUZE, "POSTSCRIPT ON THE SOCIETIES OF CONTROL"

Ethnography as Chronography

The same economic and social conditions that continue to force the mass dispersal of Filipino labor across the planet onto cruise ships, onto merchant vessels, into schools as teachers, and into homes as domestics and caregivers has also been channeling educated lower-middle- and middle-class Filipinos into the call center, or business processing outsourcing (BPO), industry within the Philippines. Unlike family and friends before them who had to migrate out of the country to find work, these tech communications workers remain in the Philippines to work. However, like their migrating counterparts in the health care and other service industries, they work in other time zones in other countries. Reuters reported in 2017 that "the BPO industry is an economic lifeline for the Philippines. It employs about 1.15 million people and, along with remittances from overseas workers, remains one of the top 2 earners of foreign exchange."[1] Yet the Reuters article also warned of the industry's imminent demise from automation. The BPO industry, an affective lifeline for the rest of the world, is yet another shifting and unpredictable economic lifeline that shapes Filipino daily life, landscapes, and futures. Rather than replacing the export labor strategy, the domestic technological offshore, as a site for corporate and marketing fantasies, adds more layers to a slew of national futures and aspirations.

Export and offshore labor markets thrive alongside one another to compete for the Filipino subject's desires to locate themselves in the future.

In an ethnography I carried out in Manila and Cebu, when call center demand was on the rise in 2011–2012 and nursing demand on the wane, I asked Shane, a call center agent, how he got into the industry, given that he had just obtained a degree in nursing. Like some other agents I interviewed, Shane studied nursing, but the demand for nurses in the United States had diminished in favor of other occupations within the health industry, like occupational and physical therapy. Shane's relatives, already practicing nurses in Los Angeles, were asking him to immigrate to the United States, he reported. However, the process was taking too long because he was not a direct relation, so to improve his prospects of emigrating, when the United States still had a shortage, only a few years earlier, he decided to take up nursing. He had just finished his Philippine nursing board exams when he was accosted at a mall by a recruiter: "When I was with my friend, we were just strolling around the mall [and] someone mentioned: Would you like to have a job?"[2] The job was at one of the big call center companies. The onerous bureaucratic process to migrate to the United States as well as the long wait time for professional credentialing abroad became opportunities for the BPO industry to reorient his future. Two global labor market demands with differing timelines overlapped to vie for Shane's and many others' economic life choices.

Call center enclaves providing offshore operations for transnational corporations glow at night in the central business districts of Manila and Cebu and in smaller towns wherever the industry can find English-speaking nocturnal denizens. The IT and Business Processing Association of the Philippines (IT-BPAP) states that the industry generated $25 billion in 2019, just behind the $33.5 billion in remittances brought in by the 10 percent of the population that works overseas and sends money back to families.[3] In addition to the four hundred thousand offshore denizens in contact centers, Rey Untal, president and CEO of the International Business Association of the Philippines (IBAP), observed in 2018 that "because of what we call the multiplier effect wherein for every job that we create, we are in fact indirectly impacting other jobs in other industries, we are collectively now employing, directly and indirectly, close to 5 million people."[4] Generating controlled and commoditized three-hundred-second (five-minute) offshore relationships, the average handling time of each call, between Filipino agents and global North consumers, over 60 percent from the United States, outsourced service voices bring small human moments into consumers' homes. The human touch from the global South is the putative voice and "soul" of the corporations that Deleuze identifies in our society of control.

While the previous chapter explored opportunity as a set of chronic assessments of changing conditions, this chapter interrogates how this new technological industry produces an affective sphere in which national subjects working offshore negotiate uneven futures and disruptions to daily and communal life. Speaking with call center agents, managers, trainers, and an industry lobbyist, I ask how they engage with various durations of time, from the three-hundred-second phone call to shifting visions of the future. Alongside cultural and discourse analysis, this ethnographic fieldwork renders visible "how the 'big events' of history are experienced by ordinary people in daily life," as the Caribbean literary critic Shalini Puri asserts, by "engaging with *people* who utter texts and with contexts that move them." She challenges literary and cultural critics to go beyond "knowing" various scales of "big events" and the "quiet everyday" toward "imagining" the "scale as lived reality." For Puri, "fieldwork invites us to achieve a textured and embodied knowledge of place."[5] In her own work, Puri identifies how personal accounts give depth and thickness to place. If imagination is structured by place in continual contestation with local and global forces, I would extend this further to argue that ethnography in cultural criticism might also serve as a chronography, a thick and textured accounting of time that captures the vernacular feel and friction not only of place as a temporality but also of timely durations in the offshore, stretching from the three-hundred-second calls and graveyard shifts to personal and global futures.

Scholarly work on call centers in India and the Philippines has been important in illuminating the production of the offshore tech worker and the attendant gender, sexual, and class formations accompanying the fantasy of national development. National, transnational, and global capital imagine variously, but not necessarily incommensurately, the place of the offshore and its potential denizens hurled toward capitalist futures. Purnima Mankekar's *Unsettling India* reads national and personal aspirations as a futurity affecting behavior and choices made by national subjects.[6] Kalindi Vora's *Life Support* argues how the flow of vital energies from the global South to the global North conditions this aspiration for futures on these different scales.[7] Specifically dealing with Philippine call centers, Alinaya Fabros's *Outsourceable Selves* provides an ethnography of call centers and details how the industry creates subjects that must adjust their bodies to continual temporal shifts and work pacing to accommodate the quotidian of global North consumers and corporations.[8] Jan Padios's insightful work *Nation on the Line* shows how "Filipino/American relatability" thrusts the Philippine colonial past into the national vision of its future. By revaluating this forced discipline, rooted in the history of the Philippines under US rule, this presumed cultural relatability by human capital makes the Philippines a key transnational player in the technological circuits of capital.[9] This fantasy, founded upon a violent history, further sediments an exceptionalism that continues to erase uneven power relations in terms of local class formations. These scholars describe the coterminous devaluation of feminized service labor and the outsourcing of peripheral repetitive labor to racialized labor offshore. In doing so, the industry makes invisible the social inequities and labor necessary to create compliant subjects from whose reproductive labor surplus value could be extracted. Furthermore, these aspirations toward global visibility obscure the localized negotiations and struggles against these multiscalar fantasies around national and corporate futures.

During the shift from nursing to BPO labor market demand in 2011–2012, I interviewed around two dozen call center workers and industry advocates in Manila and Cebu. Rather than describe exclusively the corporate and national disciplines that conjure the offshore as time and place, I hoped to get a sense of how Filipinos in the industry negotiated these overlapping durations—narratives around the national past, present, and future on which the industry relies—in their daily lives. In Manila, most of the interviews took place early in the morning, "dinner" break for the agents, in a Starbucks downstairs from a call center in the tony central business district of Makati. In Cebu, I conducted group interviews early in the morning, in a small restaurant inside a tech park composed of then newly built office buildings with fast food eateries on the street level. I begin this chapter with a reading of a BPO industry publication, *After Call* magazine, marketed to potential workers, to identify how it imagines and brands the new breed of offshore citizens emerging on its literal and metaphorical shores. The chapter then highlights the voices of Filipinos who work in the industry: Carla, Shane, Boy, Gina, and Jane from Manila and Ben and Carlo from Cebu, call center agents; Dan, a manager from Cebu; Rina, a call center trainer; and Tess, an industry spokesperson for BPAP. Based in Manila, Tess and Rina provide insight into how industry fantasies and anxieties produce and manage these offshore denizens. The call center agents and managers offer how they contextualize, understand, and inhabit these conflicting forces across varying durational scales ranging from their call habits to their daily life and their imagined future. Toward this chronography, they also articulate sites of timely frictions that give rise to desires and tactical practices that steal away and conjure time for themselves, even in spaces already occupied by fantasies that have already conjured them.[10]

Living Here: Imagining Offshore

> They are too poor to escape the reality of their lives; and they are
> too poor to live properly in the place where they live, which is the
> very place you, the tourist, want to go—so when the native sees you,
> the tourists, they envy you, they envy your ability to leave your own
> banality and boredom.
>
> Jamaica Kincaid, A Small Place

At the height of the call center boom, on the cover of *After Call* magazine, a beautiful mestiza model, well coiffed, glistening wet, and bejew-
eled, emerges from the water like Venus *sans* clamshell (Figure 1). *After
Call* was a short-lived magazine created by a national lobby organization,
the Business Processing Association of the Philippines (BPAP; now known
as IT-BPAP), produced as a recruiting tool for the industry and found in
twenty-four-hour cafes in small, glittering, caffeinated and nicotined enclaves of clubs, bars, and restaurants. BPAP, in cooperation with inves-
tors and the Philippine government, had been pushing for the industry
to train and employ more qualified Filipinos: "The demand is there; we
just need to supply them," reported Tess, a BPAP spokesperson.[11] The cover
image of a popular mestiza model/actor offers to the potential agent-
reader a visual, daytime, and bodily rather than an aural, nocturnal,
disembodied rendering of herself in postwork fantasy.[12] The model is
identifiably a call center agent, decidedly *not* working. She seems to be
on vacation: Her headset is disconnected yet still wrapped inexplicably
about her neck. Playing on the idea of an offshore agent, she is indeed off
the Philippine shores, a sexualized feminine ideal outdoors in all her sar-
torial and sexual excess. Her divine emergence is the promise of global
capitalism, but her destination remains on local shores.

Given her affective production and orientation toward global North
shores, the offshore subject would seem to refer to serviceable voices just
beyond the borders of a rich nation. For global North consumers, the offshore agent is a disembodied empathetic voice for a transnational firm.
Her "offshoreness" names the labor of creating a feeling of proximity and
propinquity to the consumer. As an empath, she is to mute both her difference and her distance—which might mean the same thing from the caller's
point of view—and address irate callers' needs with culturally appropriate
responses. Thus the seamlessness between land and sea that the offshore
agent endeavors to produce in this offshoreness also performs her erasure
from the center of capital. As Vora observes, a call is deemed successful
when the agent is able to absent herself to achieve the "seamlessness"

FIGURE 1. Cover of *After Call* magazine.

between corporation and consumer.[13] In three hundred seconds, the Filipino agent must identify the problem, pinpoint the caller's personality, deploy a rhetorical strategy, implement a logistical solution, and sustain the brand loyalty of the global North, often American, consumer. Those three hundred seconds are vital: The global production-consumption cycle must be kept in motion. Through the flows of technological circuitry, these intermittent connections follow an archipelagic logic, as Brian Roberts and Michelle Stephens have argued in the Caribbean context, "a logic within which intermittent locales assume spatial forms."[14] While "offshore" for the global North describes labor "elsewhere," somewhere off *its* coast, officially, "the Philippines claim that the waters in between and around the islands, and extending outward to a parametric boundary line, are their national waters."[15] This perspectival shift reclaims the real and metaphorical space of the offshore not as liminal but as national territory ready to be settled by a new breed of Filipino cosmopolites.

After Call envisages the offshore agent in her national and bodily form, not aural formlessness, as in her nocturnal work life, or absent abroad, like her cousins but right here at home on reconfigured shores. The publication's tagline descriptor, "The Look and Feel of the Outsourcing Industry," borrows from UX (user experience) language in digital and website design.[16] The lifestyle magazine seems to serve as a user's manual to the life of outsourced labor, so she might have the look and feel of a Philippine cosmopolite. Indeed, the magazine is not about work at all but about her *look* and *feel*, her beauty and pleasure, her visual and haptic life—senses that corporate metrics have no use for during the night. *After* the call is where and when her modeling of national citizenship happens. Her recreational time is about the reshaping of national geographies and cosmopolitan identities. *After* the call, she is supposed to reintegrate her body, her senses, her needs, and her social citizenship as a middle-class consumer of leisure. Inside the magazine, the cover model's pleasure is elaborated with a photo spread of swimwear and the season's top beach getaways in the Philippines: "Here are four quick junkets. They're only about two hours away from Manila either by land, sea or air. That's faster than braving the weekend traffic to the usual quick weekend getaway. These four escape routes will get you out of Manila faster than your longest call. So bring out the weekend warrior and book the trip."[17] Once disconnected, the national industry reorients the offshore subject bodily to the coastal shores of the archipelago as a domestic tourist.

Organizations like BPAP offer the nationalist argument that these digital communication jobs keep citizens at home where they belong while still servicing the global economy. Aware of the pull of work abroad, lobbyists offer the call center industry as the solution to Philippine economic woes and to the mass outmigration of educated working populations away from their families.

In their Facebook page, BPAP, the magazine's producer, calls on young people to "WORK ABROAD, LIVE HERE" (Figure 2) as a solution to outmigration.[18] Addressing both nationalist desires and capitalist demands

FIGURE 2. BPAP advertisement.

by creating jobs domestically, "Work Abroad, Live Here" articulates a spatial compromise to promise a redemptive status for those who work at
night away from families—not with an alternative sociality but with a
consumer lifestyle to define the terms of their national belonging. While
the slogan introduces the antonymic relationship between "abroad" and
"here," it elides the rupture between work and family life that the time
shift has introduced for many young people by figuring the terms as a false
binary *like* "here" and "abroad." In this industry of young flexible labor,
neither the spatial border moves through their bodies, as in formal colo-
nialism, nor do bodies move through borders to become ethnic bodies,
as in labor migration. Skipping the inconveniences of airports, visas, and
immigration reviews, one can indeed be at two places at once: enjoy the
glamour of working "abroad" while living "here." However, this tagline
is not immune to playful misreadings that keep the various labor markets at play. Tess, the BPAP spokesperson, observes that "for most people,
they just read 'Work abroad.' They don't read the 'live here.' Or they say,
'Work abroad, leave here . . . Long *e*'s and short *i*'s. They get confused once
again. Very Filipino."[19] In Taglish, the vernacular mix of Tagalog and English, pronouncing the *i* as a long *e* plays with accents, since the *e-i* vowel
in Filipino renders these sounds interchangeable. Therefore *living* in the
Philippines is heard at the same time as *leaving* the Philippines. The mes-

sage cancels itself out. However, what might be "very Filipino" is not the misunderstanding at all but the intentional misreading of the corporate message. The pull to "leave" pronounced with a long *e* remains strong for many. Given the misreadings and mishearings, BPAP has since abandoned the "Work Abroad, Live Here" tagline.

Rather than inhabiting the global North's liminal "elsewhere," the BPO industry has created an imaginative space for this new inhabitant of the night who answers the call to remain in and true to the Philippines. The magazine offers an alternative class geography and identity that offers a "way out" of social and economic stasis without leaving Philippine shores. The way out is to stay in. The offshore identity here indexes the cosmopolitan aspirations of a class of people who could potentially have income and social mobility. The BPAP representation of the offshore agent reterritorializes her as a national subject, a hedonistic one who looks to her own shores for her pleasure. Corporate nationalism offers a visual and economically advantageous solution to what Campomanes and Gonzalez have signaled as a problematic in Filipino and Filipino diasporic expressions around multiple dislocations: "to negotiate and map their 'communities' in the space of conflicting demands between 'a national longing for form' and a radically (anti)national predicament of formless dispersals."[20] Decidedly not a migrant or overseas worker, a native islander, a peasant, or a domestic here or abroad, the offshore subject is cosmopolitan, and though barely leaving the shores of the Philippines, she is part of the consuming middle class that, like the elite and foreign tourists, can buy leisure time. Constructed as a nationalist by not migrating out of the physical confines of nation, her assimilation to a foreign culture lends her an air of international sophistication, unlike the *balikbayan* (Filipino returnee) or overseas worker, who has to live as a racialized migrant. Offshore but at home, she can skirt the issues of racialization and national borders faced by her overseas or migrating counterparts. The offshore agent, as an emergent national *and* transnational subject, is the product of a union between call center companies producing denizens of corporate time at night and national industry lobbyists producing consumer citizens during the day.

Through temporal migration into "IT parks" and "tech centers," the industry offers offshore agents some of the economic means by which to "live properly in the place where they live," transformed in the industry magazine's pages into "the very place you, the tourist, want to go."[21] Ruled and measured as she is by several chronic and spatial attachments, the offshore agent as a liminal figure simulates being in sync as a sonic presence with corporate global time at night while living bodily in Philippine national time. She embodies the tensions of inhabiting a global telematic circuitry. As Raka Shome argues in her work on Indian call centers: "The present itself is multiply extended across geographies, nations, spaces through telematic communication, and it is this collision of times stretched over multiple geographies and spatial relations in one moment that creates the diasporic tension and articulates the subject as hybrid."[22] The con/fusion of temporal belonging creates the offshore as a specific corporate-national space. But this emergence of temporal rather than spatial migration so that Filipinos might serve the global North provides a different spin on dispersal and on the hybridity not of a people but of their everyday.

Leaving Here:
Harnessing the Past in Three Hundred Seconds

I arrived at Carla's home in Manila at 9 AM. Carla had arrived home from her shift a few hours ago. She was already quite busy with her children and new grandchild. Carla was in her forties, but her petite frame and young-looking face did not make her stand out from her younger co-workers, mostly between twenty-one and thirty-five years old, though they refer to her with the affectionate honorific "Mama." Like the cover model, Carla usually worked at night from 8 PM to 5 AM, with changing night shifts every few months. Her day off allowed her to spend time with me for the interview while catching up with her children and the day's household chores. Unlike the model, Carla lived in the nongated part of inner-city Manila, in a small, modest house and small lot that had seen better days. The wooden house that had stood at the site was a typical old-style Filipino urban home, elevated from the street, but it had burned down a few years ago and suffered more damage from recent hurricanes. With two years of college under her belt, she began working at a major call center company four years ago, two of them servicing a US phone company and the last year and half with a US cable company.

When I requested an interview with Carla, she repeatedly requested that we conduct the interview in Tagalog or Taglish because she was so tired of speaking English that "*dinudugo na ang ilong ko*" (my nose is bleeding), a colloquial Tagalog phrase humorously used to indicate an aversion to being forced to speak or listen to English at length.[23] Once the colonial language forced on peoples across dozens of Philippine ethnolinguistic groups, global English had now become the language of work for many but certainly not the language of casual conversation or intimate feelings. English was a wearisome commodity tailored for work. Taglish, by contrast, allowed for linguistic play and puns that covered a range of emotions. She hoped that our conversation would feel more casual, less formal, and less tainted with workplace demands. What she requested, as with most of my interviewees, was the freedom to codeswitch or get at feelings that would require multiple languages to express. English had become a language of regulation, workplace efficiency, timed responses, correct scripting, and practiced empathy. The freedom to use a Philippine language would create in her home or around a table at Starbucks a place, duration, sociality, and affect decidedly not of offshore work.

Carla reported that the phone company with whom the call center contracted paid her well because the account required not only technical knowledge but also a "strong personality." Call center companies would prescreen potential agents not simply for English-language proficiency but, more importantly, for behavioral competencies, favoring those with forceful personalities who can deal with American callers. In her job interview, Carla observed that they were "looking to see how you carry yourself and if you have a strong personality because *kausap mo Americano*" (you will be speaking with Americans). A strong personality meant that the agent could be "dominant" and "aggressive": "[Callers might] curse you, but they train you *papano ikaw mag-dominate sa call*" (how you can dominate the call). Furthermore, the English language–skills exam during the interview also served as a behavioral test to determine if the worker had the confidence and assertiveness presumed to match that of the American callers the industry served.

At the point in time I conducted these interviews, the Philippines had just become the number-one nation in voice operations, thanks to an English-speaking population that continued to imbibe American culture over its hundred-plus-year-long colonial and neocolonial relationship with the United States. "Filipino/American relatability," as Jan Padios has termed this connection, had become "social capital and cultural resource fueling the Philippines' neoliberal aspirations."[24] By the end of 2011, the Philippines had outpaced India in growth and number for voice operations.[25] Indian-owned companies like Aegis moved operations into the Philippine archipelago. In fact, in a rhetorical move whereby the Orient orientalizes other parts of the Orient, the chief executive of the Mumbai-based Aegis has described the Philippines as "a unique combination of Eastern, attentive hospitality and attitude of *care and compassion* mixed with what I call Americanization."[26] The marketing justification fused and confused historical imperialism with ahistorical sociality to generate the soul of corporations. At the same time, the belief buttresses a Philippine affective exceptionalism circulated as commodity to reproduce "a form of Philippine, as well as U.S., exceptionalism."[27]

While the local industry elites would tout this cultural past as an asset, the notion of an inherent character of "care and compassion" from the individual agents was far from given, might in fact be a thing of the past, and would need refurbishment. As Tess, the lobby spokesperson, warned: "So, even though we say that service is inherent in the Filipino culture, we need to make sure that we continue to monitor this, because the generation of today—it's different. Everything is online. So, the interpersonal interaction might disappear if we don't continue to measure it and to nurture it."[28] In her estimation, because the young denizens of the industry tended to inhabit and had become habituated to the world of texting, Instagram, Facebook, and other social media, their caring, interpersonal skills might have been blunted. Thus, the ragged vestiges of the supposed national character might in fact be a thing of the past and must be rendered usable for the future only after being processed and refined through precise measures and behavioral monitoring. In other words, caring and Filipino/American relatability did not come naturally but needed to be cultivated. It was not so much the so-called innate warmth of Filipinos that made for successful call center agents but the filtering, casting, and training process that cultivated a resilient English-speaking pool of lower-middle- and middle-class workers who could talk back forcefully to American customers.

Sorry / Not Sorry in Three Hundred Seconds

What was meant by communications skills was never simply English mastery but behavior modification. Like other call center agents I interviewed, Carla related how these affective ties across oceans were produced through improvisational scripting and management training. Indeed, training and quality control in the workplace was about the continual modulation and refinement of the perceptual speed and accuracy of their responses. Tess, the industry spokesperson I interviewed, explained that the skills necessary to train college students include "learning orientation, which is your willingness to learn product and service information—courtesy, empathy, reliability, and responsiveness."[29] Rina, a trainer in a call center, would monitor and correct behavior that reflects these qualities:

> Are they expressing things in a sarcastic way? Are we able to detect that? . . . So, in order to address that, we give them drills. Like, what if the customer says this? What would you say? And then, to make

it more realistic, we would act as the customer and they act as their own selves, as agents. And then see how they do that, properly. And then we give them feedback of course. We give them suggestions."[30]

Sarcastic tones, even if unintentional during unguarded moments, serve only to distance agent from consumer. Agents are taught to "personalize" the problem, that is, perform emotional labor in the simulation of empathy. Barring actual empathy, those tones would have to be muted or replaced by stock responses. The trainer further refined this understanding of empathy as aspirational practice: "It's placing the customer—it's placing yourself in the shoes of the customer and what they're feeling at the time—what they're experiencing . . . there's just a misconception of empathy being equal to 'I'm sorry,' or being a means of apologizing for everything and anything."[31] Companies would often provide cultural training before starting on a new account so that agents understood and were familiar with the parameters for their improvisational scripting. From the trainer's official standpoint, effective agents should be able to feel foreign callers' frustrations and anger so that the empathy might go beyond the words spoken on the phone and achieve some sort of genuine reaching out during that three-hundred-second drama. Resolution would emerge from true understanding between human beings.

When queried about their one week of cultural training with different aspects of American culture, Boy responded: "The cultural training [is] more like call listening activities. We get to listen to how they would react. And we're given sample spiels in order for us to help [with] rebuttal if ever they would say something—especially how to handle irate customers, how to pacify them, how to build rapport with the customers."[32] About 80 to 90 percent of the calls required customer care agents to "calm" customers, as usually the calls involved a billing or technical issue. The semblance of empathy was therefore scripted toward what might calm the average American psychology. When I asked how he would handle an irate American caller, he continued: "There is actually a certain process, but normally they would say positive scripting, that's how it goes—we empathize with them all of the time, we provide a sense of urgency. So, before the call ends, we empathize; that's part of our process." In practice, "We always say sorry even if there's no need to say sorry at all."[33]

BOY: "I know what you've been through."
SHANE: *Ganyan.* [Like that.] *'Yang mga ganyan. Bola lang.* [Like that. Just b.s.]
BOY: Just to make them feel that you're really there to help them. To calm them.

SHANE: You have to make it sound as if you care for that person, but you care because you care for your scorecard and yourself. You have to "fake it" that you care, that you are helping them. Of course it depends on the customer. If it is a grandmother, the Filipino comes out and I genuinely want to help. We're—we're good at faking it—

SHANE: You just need to make sure that your tone of voice—

BOY: I think we're already veterans in faking. When your team leader's listening, sometimes, they'll say, "Oh, you did not empathize." Something like that. So, over time, you tend to just use the generic scripting. And since it's already part of the system, or it's a part of you, you can do—you can say it with, like, feelings, but deep inside, it's just—you're doing it for the sake of your scorecard. Because you would not pass the quality [control].

Absent of any real desire to help, as with a grandmother, in Shane's example, agents would deploy generic phrases and controlled tones to get at the desired empathic result: "I apologize," "I'm more than happy to help you with this issue," "Don't worry," "I know what you've been through," "I would feel the same way." For some agents, empathy in practice might be as simple as repeating those learned phrases, which become part of the agent's "American" repertoire, provided by but wielded in contrast to the trainer's aspiration for genuine connection in each and every call. Rather than resolution, assurance as a goal was about producing a semblance of being "there" for the customer to "calm" the caller.

For Boy, if the scripting had become "part of the system or it's part of you," then the system and "you" had also become indistinguishable in his agent persona. Boy admitted: "When you're in a call, there's something in you that, you know, makes you like, an American already. 'Cause you really need to be like them, for them to, you know, for you to connect."[34] This self-observation about absorbing a system echoes Mankekar's observations about the call center as a practice that could unsettle the "binary between impersonation and personation, and fictive versus authentic identity."[35] Keeping his livelihood would dictate that his corporate and personal goals converge, yet this elsewhere "deep inside" as the frictive location belies the import of the question around authenticity in the first place. I am not so much concerned with whether intimate connections "actually" happened but rather with what techniques and desires drive agents to produce the desired effect. As Boy pointed out, the training allowed him as the agent to generate a response good enough to pass quality control. If his mood or other conditions were not right to deliver empathy, as was often the case, falling back on tried-and-true technique would save the day, his nightly scorecards, and his job. Boy's misdirected trajectory of care "for the sake of your scorecard" would locate that space "deep inside" to add nuance to the blurring between "fictive" and "authentic." In the unfolding drama of the call, the agent might care about the scorecard and monthly averages, making the *effect* the same but not the affective *direction*. The direction of care would point toward self-preservation, that is, a job tomorrow. Customer calm and satisfaction might simply be the fortuitous byproduct. While not so much about resisting corporate mandates but rather about operating within its measured constraints, this affective diversion recognizes a self-aware subjectivity distanced from the customer and corporate demands. Producing the illusion of seamlessness might serve industry goals. However, self-erasure through the mimicry of script and self-transformation into a persona do not necessarily mean alignment and synchronicity with corporate demands.

Agents' accounts relate how they navigate those three-hundred-second calls in ways that give lie to the presumed fidelity of workers to a social formation afforded by any one industry. When asked what agents disliked most about their jobs, not surprisingly, most mentioned that they hated the calls, or, more specifically, the repetitive nature of the calls:

> SHANE: I don't like the calls. *Ayoko ng* calls. . . . Our job itself—let's say every five minutes, you get the same issue again and again. Sometimes, *nakakasawa na. Parang, bakit 'yon na lang palagi? Paulit-ulit na lang. Paulit-ulit. Minsan, nakakainis na—* something like that. [Sometimes, you get sick of it. It's like, why is it the same thing over and over? It's just repetitive. Repetitive. Sometimes, it's just annoying.][36]

In the face of the global North's repetitive ire, the agents' emotions range from indifference to genuine care to annoyance. Hanging up on irate callers would result in disciplinary action, but disconnecting abusive callers, sending them into sonic oblivion, was a commonplace practice. One agent reported, "*Hinahayaan ko lang silang magsalita. Minu-mute ko lang siya*" (I just let them talk. I just mute them).[37] When a caller goes on a rant, agents might simply mute the noise. In fact, while the agent's disappearance might be the desired effect to make the call "seamless," as corporate guidelines would mandate, the agent absenting herself in this way, so as not to be affected by the continual complaints, served the same end, while also reclaiming time and personal energies. Annoyance perhaps reveals the timely frictions "deep inside" through which the disciplined subject modulates and shifts these affective energies, as a refusal to be in synch with work time.

The human capacity to feel friction in the repetitive nature of the calls suggests automation as a solution, since by most accounts AI technology does not yet feel tedium when faced with the banality of global North concerns. Intimacy with strangers half a world away is performed in five-minute spurts, ten to twelve times per hour for seven hours, repeated an average of seventy to eighty times by each agent every night and through the dawn. International call center companies must continually mold, train, and measure the performance of offshore agents to generate empathetic responses, not skills, for corporate clients. Increased demands for efficiency in an industry of repetitive responses will likely turn to artificial intelligence (AI) and automation. "In the next 3–5 years it will really be hitting harder. It will be there, it will be a reality, this AI," projected Socioeconomic Planning Secretary Ernesto Pernia in early 2018.[38] The BPO industry may be about to plateau, he warned. If global capital makes automatons of workers, then real automatons would make for better workers. The so-called sunrise industry, like other industries before it, shift with the global North's economic demands. Like nursing before it, the technical work of the BPO industry, these offerings of the everyday and the future, is part of a series of overlapping and shifting narratives, unkept promises, and failed aspirations that continue to redirect workers' lives, careers, and daily life.

Tactical and Contaminated Futures

Carla's life was redirected when she saw the advertisement for call center work "by accident," she said, when interviewing for another job in the southern part of Manila. Her seeing the job notice was in fact not accidental but evidence of the ubiquity and aggressive placement of industry ads. The BPO advertisements were everywhere in lower-middle- to middle-class malls, schools and colleges, local airports, even some upscale neighborhoods, locations where a population with some college education might congregate to shop, eat, study, or travel. The advertisements littered the city, and my informants all knew friends and relatives who had been recruited into the industry: "It was like almost everyone was getting into call centers, and I heard it was actually paying good," said one.[39] What the industry afforded these potential workers, who already had the education but perhaps occupied a precarious middle-class status, was a fiscal power that otherwise might be beyond reach without proper family and social connections. With a minimum two to four years of college, the agent could make approximately 23,000 Philippine pesos ($500) per month, a considerable amount for a college-educated Filipino without job experience. After social security and healthcare deductions, Carla was usually left with 11,000 to 15,000 pesos ($220 to $300) per month, a decent though not extravagant wage in Manila, given her children and a new grandchild to care for in her household.

Recruitment of agents can be quite aggressive, since the competition for educated, English-speaking workers comes not only from migratory industries like nursing and other health-related fields but also from other call center companies. Gina recounted that she was walking out of one interview for a call center when she was approached by her current company. Knowing she had just come from another interview, they convinced her to have a talk with them at a nearby fast-food place. Companies found it difficult to keep their agents from going from one company to another, a practice known as call center hopping. The "hopper" would leave a call center site for another every six months for better pay. Given the high attrition rate, companies must continually replenish their ranks. After a brief chat, Gina took a quick diagnostic test, after which they offered her a contract, using high-pressure sales techniques, saying that the signing contract was good only for that day. However, the recruiters also wanted to make sure that she would stay for more than a year.

After a previous failed interview in which she got tripped up by a question about her "future," Gina learned that being honest about her own life goals—whether to start a career in the Philippines or elsewhere—was *not* the right answer. Gina focused on the question in the interview process that gets at longevity of commitment: "How do you see yourself within the next something? Five years—how do you see yourself in [the company]?" Much like the job, the interview process was a practice in improvised scripting. The group of agents I interviewed suggested ways to circumvent the trap of corporate futures.

> GINA: You cannot really tell. That's the future, *'di ba? Pero* you have to answer that five years from now, I can be a TL, I can be a supervisor. *Parang talagang*—positive attributes *sa kanila*? [You cannot really tell. That's the future, right? But you have to answer that five years from now, I can be a TL (team leader), I can be a supervisor. Like really positive attributes for them.]
>
> JANE: *Para ma-enhance mo 'yong* capability—*'yong* ability *mo*—with their help. You have the abilities, you know you were able to finish your degree and all that, but *hindi mo siya na-a-*apply, so you need someone *parang, 'di ba*? [So you can enhance your capabilities,

your abilities. You have the abilities. You know you were able to finish your degree and all that, but you couldn't use your degree, so you need them, right?][40]

The agents were pragmatic about the idea of a "future," the future being, by definition, indeterminate. Whether or not the agents believed the corporate progress narrative, they understood that a prepared response would get them out of the question of the "future trap." Industry employers were aware that the candidates' education and training were never intended for the BPO industry. Usually candidates had been trained in nursing, commerce, tourism, engineering, or marketing, as was the case with all my informants. However, the "correct" answer to the "trick question" about their future was to say that the company would make the most of the skills she had already acquired. The call center company could provide the right opportunities to use and develop skills she had so that she might grow with the company. The immediate goal during the interview was to get the job with good pay while waiting for a visa clearance or for professional credentials to go abroad. Paying lip service to corporate fantasies was a means to an end.

Center hopping and practiced responses for interviews remain some of the survivalist tactics necessary to tide the agent over from one opportunity to the next while keeping several possible futures in play. Filipinos navigate the future offshore, a capitalist reimagining of the national space, as one of a long line of disruptive and improvisational futures for themselves. The ready access to higher pay in the industry makes it easier both in terms of time and resources for a family member to contribute to household expenses and support younger siblings through their education.

> SHANE: So, I really miss nursing. *Kaso, iniisip ko lang, parang,* if I'll go back to nursing, *parang* back to zero *na naman kasi ulit.* [But I was thinking, if I go back to nursing, it's like going back to zero again.] I don't want to start again. Especially since I'm already helping my family.[41]

Meeting immediate needs makes possible long-term goals. Pursuing the nursing route would entail more time with little or no salary to gain work experience at local hospitals, often done for little or no pay, and more waiting time to get through domestic and foreign migration bureaucracies.

The industry would like to represent BPOs as a viable and easier alternative to migration by foregrounding consumer citizenship as a claim to nationalism and national belonging. A feature article announces an emerging socioeconomic formation: "BPOs: The New Middle Class." The article optimistically and encouragingly reports:

> In a nutshell, what the report says is that the BPO industries is one of the main pillars of the Philippines GDP growth, and this is for the expansion of the country's middle class over the past decade. A strong middle class is what the country needs to grow more and display stellar economic performance. The BPO industry is supplying exactly this, but what does it take to be in the middle class? Is the average BPO bear really a member of this club?

The short piece goes on to cite quantitative national criteria from the National Statistical Coordination Board for the trappings of middle-class status in the Philippines, including an "annual income ranging between PhP 251,283 ($6,282) to PhP 2,045,280 ($51,132), live in a domicile made of strong materials, a refrigerator, and a radio."[42] Radios notwithstanding, BPO workers from call center agents to managers can earn anywhere from $300 to $2,000 per month, quite within the enormously wide middle-class range provided by the article. The anxiety to prove through statistical numbers that the reader belonged to this socioeconomic class or "club" permeates the article as well as the advertisements for affordable condos and vacations filling the pages of the magazine. Being part of the industry and of the expansion of the middle class, the writer implied, was to be a main pillar in Philippine national growth and development.

Yet the bodily representation of the call center agent as a youthful, rich pleasure seeker also evinced social and cultural anxieties around the new middle class. By paying such high wages in a nontraditional occupation, the industry shifted the notion of fiscal power being the domain of land-owning families or of the colonial bureaucracy and controlled by professional credentialing at accredited universities. Call center firms and companies provided much of the industry training, not universities. Part of the cultural anxiety then lies in fiscal power acquired not through the traditional channels established by a colonial history of higher education or an elite family network. Informants pointed to the perceived ease and lack of professional credentials, like a bachelor's degree, required for positions in the industry.

> DAN: I think they would say that it is easy to be recruited into a call center but it's actually not.
> BEN: [They] think it makes you dumber because of the repetitiveness.

CARLO: You don't need a bachelor's degree to get into the call center.
DAN: Only two years is needed.[43]

The agents' chosen or compelled jobs at call centers did not follow the (neo)colonial routes to middle-class respectability (for example, doctor, lawyer, engineer, teacher, or nurse), particularly because institutional credentialing or imprimaturs have seemingly been bypassed. While commanding the attributes of the privileged with fraught "global" or "lightly accented" English, some college education, and much purchasing power, these offshore workers do not necessarily have the family and elite educational institutional network of other middle-class subjects. In *Working the Night Shift*, Reena Patel had similarly observed this manner of social devaluation of female labor in call centers in India. Not only was this feminized work deemed available to anyone with minimal skills, but many women felt "part of the backlash that workers experience for not paying their dues and instead enjoy[ing] a salary level that was previously available to an even narrower segment of the population (that is professional, white-collar workers)."[44] Padios's work on the Philippine call centers underscored how the call center stigma devalued the very attributes of education, wealth, and body grooming that the elite relied on as traditional status markers.[45] Their cosmopolitanism simulates and values the promise of the foreign, to use Vicente Rafael's term, without having to leave the country.[46] However, these digital denizens are not legible as returnees (*balikbayan*) from overseas who have accumulated some wealth, a now-common phenomenon dating from the 1970s. Hence, these cyberpark citizens who come from such dangerous proximity to the "offshore" seem to threaten a social-class order with promiscuity of a different sort: class promiscuity.[47]

This anxiety was apparent among a group of call center agents and managers I interviewed in Cebu one very early morning over "dinner" after their shifts. Occupying various posts as agents, team leaders, and managers, the agents were only too aware of the way many perceive their membership in "the club" of respectable middle-classness.

DAN: But it was my choice—it was my decision. . . . It's been always normal [for] Filipinos that they would look down on call centers although they know that it's a high-paying job. . . . They would say, "Why only a call center—why did you not choose your own profession?" But if you come to think of it: yes, you are a manager in a bank, but your pay! Mine is 40 or 50 percent higher than yours. But I'm a manager here, too. So that's the big difference.[48]

While the BPO worker had fiscal power and the same managerial title, he had no social status as a call center agent. A lower-paid bank manager, however, was perceived to have chosen a respectable career track because it was a recognized occupation. One could even "major" in finance or business administration as a proper route to respectability. According to my interviewees, others outside the industry felt that working as a call center agent was meant to be a temporary job before the worker secures a "real" or more permanent "career" in the Philippines or abroad. When asked why they stay in such stressful and competitive jobs, the agents expressed ambivalence around staying on as well-paid but not well-respected urban professionals. Consuming power could not cleanse the agent of her class origins and reveals instead her tenuous hold on middle-class respectability. Proper and respectable futures could not possibly be found in the industry, which has no colonial or national history and is not recognized by universities, except perhaps at lower-tier trade schools.

Aside from the pay differential, the temporal shift also constructed a difference around morality and cultural belonging. When someone in the group interview would use terms such as "normal" and "vampire" to describe daytime and nighttime BPO workers, respectively, the rest would smile, chuckle, or simply nod in agreement at the colorful description. While the call center industry offers a way for families to stay together in the same country, inhabitants of the offshore do not necessarily share the same circadian and quotidian rhythms as other citizens to make traditional family life a reality. They no longer participate in reunions and other life-occasion markers. For many agents I interviewed, shared waking hours with family were decidedly not spent on sand and surf but in playing catch-up with duties to children and other family members. Their families would adjust to the agents' frequent absences and accommodate their sleeping and eating cycles, including creating special sleeping quarters in darkened, air-conditioned, and noise-free parts of the house. Though physically present, they are often secreted away and asleep during the family activities their income has made possible. Because of economic demands, these young workers violate this central duty of communality and sense of belonging, substituting a physical dislocation offshore with more of an exile from the everyday. Even when disconnected from the global circuitry, the agents' disconnection extends to their own families.

Working at night as "vampires" or "daywalkers," away from their families and friends and unlike "normal" people, negatively affected others' perception of the agents' morals and values.[49] My informants seemed to

understand that many see them as youths living a culture of permissive-
ness with plenty of disposable income and carousing into the night and
early morning hours. Never mind that the night and early morning co-
incided with their working and postwork hours. Others, they felt, saw
them as tolerating or partaking in nonmarital and nonheterosexual sex,
accompanied by excessive smoking and drinking. In the group interview,
one said, "They think you keep drugs because you have a lot of money."
"Or that you have AIDS," continued another.[50] Even in the news media,
call center agents would be characterized as promiscuous and even a main
source of the spread of sexually transmitted diseases. The year before, a
news report made a splash in the local news about the rise in absolute
numbers of HIV cases and STIs.[51] The rise was then with little scientific
evidence linked to call center agents and their presumed promiscuity as
young nighttime workers.

These slights, based on social status and shading into opprobrium
around sexual and social morality, seek to delegitimize the offshore as a
site of a futurity. The stigma of having or being associated with HIV/AIDS
assailed the legitimacy of a future dependent on the industry. Such anti-
sex and homophobic accusations marked their bodies as not having a
future, and if they had any at all it was already pathologically, even culturally, contaminated. When asked about this perception, one responded:
"[They think] we don't get to follow the old Filipino way because we were
talking with Americans."[52] Since the agents worked in the very visible
gleam of the call center areas of the city, this visual separation exacerbated the anxieties around the nocturnal character of the offshore lifestyle. These young people, some would claim, inhabited a foreign space
and time zone, within the nation. These bright spaces at night stood for
an aberrant trajectory away from the normative expectations of national
space and time. Such a sentiment seems to assert that a generation of class
upstarts who might actually incorporate nonheterosexual or nonnormative sex in their everyday lives ought not possibly share in or even
be the future of the nation.

The agents as the offshore's inhabitants recount how the proximity of
the offshore and its potential contamination of national futures remap the
geographies and chronographies of national belonging. The offshore subject's partial dislocation reveals yet another texture and another outline
of the Philippine meta-archipelago and its "'dispersed nationality' and the
experience of multiple dislocations."[53] The offshore dislocates the national
imagination and its own image of itself even as the offshore denizens disrupt the accepted social order, from the agents' diurnal absence to their
aberrant class mobility, which lacks the traditional educational and mi-

gratory trajectories, like that of the teachers in Diaz's documentary or Sally in Alvar's short story. The offshore subject's temporal migration into the global simultaneity of times during the night shift produces otherness to nation not by leaving political borders but via an exile from the everyday and proper national futures.

Fantasy Redux

Sedimented with colonial histories already fraught with cultural anxieties and transgressions, the offshore site trades in the intermittent relationships between the Philippines and North America throughout the night. Local practices of hopping, faking, and disconnecting reveal timely ruptures in the offshore agent's nightly and repetitive "economic" performance, to echo Oscar Campomanes and N. V. M. Gonzalez, so that they might buy or steal time for themselves. The anxieties, annoyances, boredom, and pivots that fill the agents' chronography of their lives disrupt the seamless ebb and flow across the telematic circuitry.[54] While the "temporality of aspiration" places futurity as part of social formation, it is also the case that Filipinos imagine and are attuned to several futures all at once.[55] This demand for continual shifts in aspiration and scripted responses is what post-Marxist theorists like Massumi and Berardi see as distinguishing contemporary formations of capitalism from their predecessors. Post-Fordist capitalism relies on behavior modulation as a dominant mode. This differs from what Foucault has described as disciplinary (and colonial) forms found in traditional institutions like church, family, and school. Such affective shifts also comprise survivalist tactics by workers as affects of survival. The shift from disciplinary to modulatory behavior insists upon a regime of continual shifting of measures, leaving the worker to pay the bodily and emotional price of always trying to "measure up." For Deleuze, the shift from the disciplinary society that Foucault described for the eighteenth to twentieth centuries to the postwar society of control produced different subjects: from "a discontinuous producer of energy" to one who is "undulatory in orbit, in a continuous network."[56] Deleuze quips: "Everywhere surfing has already replaced the older sports."[57] The technological descriptor from his writing from the early 1990s as well as his water-sports metaphor articulate the seeming disconnect the *After Call* image insists upon: technology and nature, material shores and fluidity, sensory parts and bodily whole. Indeed, Deleuze's figurations are more apt than ever well into the twenty-first century. Read through the agents' chronography, the glamorous figure on the trade magazine's cover is less a promise and more an ominous tangle of possible dead ends, from the headset wound about her neck to her un-sure footing in the water, yet continual improvisation is what her work and nonwork life demand as tactical survival.

Nuanced by the agents' articulations of daily life and futures, the off-shore inhabitant as cover image reveals that two mechanisms have a grip on her: first, her headset potentially attaching her to global capitalism and, second, the outlines of the national development reimagined by the in-dustry's lobbyists for her future. Between her productive sensory capaci-ties for the world and her now mute, sexualized body for the nation lie the anxieties and contradictions the image seeks to allay. The visual dis-connect between the sensuous depiction of water cascading down her body and the less visible headset illustrates her double bind and the ten-sion between the technological circuitry coiled around the model's neck and her pleasure-taking and -giving body. The device that extracts her voice at night to give service and comfort to irate global North custom-ers has been disconnected, rendered powerless, only for the moment, to be sure, but is still inexplicably coiled about her as an accessory in the daytime. What do these accessories make accessible? The accessories—bathing suit, earrings, headset, the beach itself—promise access to more and endless accessories. The accessories in fact render her accessible in parts and in whole, at all hours, at different points in history. While the nation-state generates ideological structures through consumption and technology to produce subjects that conform to capital demands, these subjects negotiate and *live* with the multiple futures and continued dis-ruptions to their material lives.

Whether figured in terms of aspirational consumer embodiment or a nation plugged into global data circuitry, embedded in futurity's pleasures are doubt, precarity, contradictions, even the future's imminent and ul-timate demise, as the industry itself predicts. Short-circuits happen; the line can go dead anytime. If arrivals and middles are the concern of the first two chapters, death and precarity are the focus of the next chapter and the coda. Looking at various stagings of death in a musical, the next chapter explores how death and invisibility expand the political landscape and vocabulary of Filipino audiences and viewers.

4 / "We Have No Time to Wallow": Death and Other Timely Diversions

KAYLA: . . . hoy, kelan tayo magre-rehearse?

SHAI: Ay naku, Kayla. Maldita ka talaga. Dapat magseremonyas tayo para sa first death anniversary ni Chelsea. Kahit saan man tayo naroroon, i-synchronize natin. Alas sais ng umaga, oras sa atin.

THALIA: Teka muna, hatinggabi dito yun e.

KAYLA: May muta pa ako noon.

SHAI: Ano ba? Para kay Chelsea ito, ano!

THALIA: Bakit nga 6:00 Philippine time?

SHAI: Parang oras na nagliliwanag pa lang sa atin, tulad ni Chelsea, sunshine girl.

THALIA: "Sa atin." Ayaw mo yung nagliliwanag pa lang dito sa Israel? Tutal dito tayo nag-meet.

SHAI: Nagpapalusot ka, 'no? Sige na nga! 7 AM sa Israel. Sabihan nyo si Nonah.

KAYLA: Pota naman, tanghaling tapat dito? Sayang ang glutathion ko.

SHAI: Nagse-set pa lang tayo ng oras . . . [*With fondness*] di pa rin kayo nagbabago.

KAYLA: Joke lang. Sige . . . kahit anong oras.

JONEE: Oy, baka di yan matuloy ha. Taga sa bato yan ha.

[KAYLA: . . . Hey, when are we rehearsing?

SHAI: Oh Kayla, you're terrible. We should be serious about Chelsea's first death anniversary. No matter where we are, we should synchronize. At 6 AM, time at home (Philippines).

THALIA: Wait a minute, that's midnight here!

KAYLA: I'll still have sleep in my eye.

SHAI: What's the matter with you guys? This is for Chelsea!

THALIA: Why 6 AM Philippine time?

SHAI: So it's sunrise! Just like Chelsea, our sunshine girl!

THALIA: "At home"? Don't you prefer sunrise in Israel? After all, we all met here!

SHAI: You're trying to get one over, aren't you? OK 7 AM in Israel. You guys tell Nonah.

KAYLA: Damn it, that's almost noon here! What a waste of glutathione (skin-lightening pills)!

SHAI: We're just trying to settle on a time . . . [*with fondness*] and you haven't changed a bit.

KAYLA: I'm just kidding. All right . . . Any time.

JONEE: I hope this doesn't fall through! This is set in stone now, ok?]
(translation mine)

This dialogue takes place entirely in the dark, disembodied voices from different parts of the globe. Suddenly, the house and stage lights blaze onto a flamboyant, Las Vegas–style fantasy finale, conjuring the dead Chelsea in glamorous, sublime, musical pageantry (Figure 3). The local Manila musical *Care Divas* follows the loves and ultimate death of the protagonist Chelsea, by day a Filipino migrant worker in Israel and by night part of a lip-syncing drag troupe composed of Filipino caregivers. The finale's excess marks a separation from the musical's narrative time and place, satisfying both the musical theater form and the audience's pleasure, but it is also quite jarring. After all, the audience has just witnessed Chelsea die in a suicide bombing amid the chaos of an immigration raid, human collateral damage in the Palestinian-Israeli conflict (Figure 4). The sudden, saturating dazzle of light assaults the senses and invites audience applause; however, like the diegetic death scene, where she is left standing alone bewildered, it leaves open the "meaning" of Chelsea's abrupt end of life. For, what *is* the end? *For what* is the end? The finale offers sensory delight and humor but not logical sense. Foregrounding sensoria over sense, the musical refuses easy closure to index the impossibility of addressing adequately the structural questions and political contradictions that render her death meaningless. The sensations and emotions, including ecstatic pleasure, around death in the three final scenes focus on the audience communing in and with this untimely death. Each earth-shattering scene makes sensible the shapes and audible the resonances of various intimate and world-making communalities.[1]

FIGURE 3. Care Divas finale. (Photo by Gellin Ivy De Leon. By permission of PETA Library and Archives.)

FIGURE 4. Chelsea dies. (Photo by Gellin Ivy De Leon. By permission of PETA Library and Archives.)

Staged in Manila off and on in various venues from 2011 to 2017, always to sold-out audiences in its extended runs, *Care Divas* as a musical about queer Filipino stage performers and their performance of care in the overlapping domestic spaces of Israel and the Philippines makes manifest an emotional and sensory archive of migratory life and subjection. I focus on the sensory worlds the production imparts that transport, or perhaps more aptly in the French *sens*, redirect time and narrative to foreground unsanctioned and obscured communalities. I begin by exploring, in the musical's ending, affect's directionality as an opening to sensory worlds, which takes place alongside the director's clear refusal to wallow in sentiment. These affective diversions, in both senses of pleasure and directionality, make manifest sensorial intimacies and linked fates and offer glimpses into world-making capacities. I then trace the social context of Filipino migrants as an "invisible" population in Israel to look at the musical's source material in an earlier documentary, *Paper Dolls* (*Bubot Niyar*, 2006), directed by Tomer Heymann, initially targeted to an Israeli audience.[2] Drawing clear inspiration from the documentary, *Care Divas* is not so much a musical version of the film but a direct response to the documentary's emphatically sentimental attention to local Israeli family and national politics. Finally, I examine the musical's radical diversion from and political response to the source material by confounding normative social alignments assumed in migrant family obligations and occupational care work to think through other social formations within these. Together these diversions, like the iterative but itinerant final scenes, direct us not to timeless utopias but to time sensorially transformed.

Refusal to Wallow

The musical opens with Chelsea and her intimate father-child relationship with her Israeli employer, Isaac.[3] By stark contrast, the next scene explores the disquiet of her friend and roommate Shai, who is continually haunted by his overbearing mother and family in the Philippines, who depend heavily on him as their primary source of income. The plot pits the cheery younger Chelsea with the jaded, older Shai, each of their emotional lives oriented in different national directions. Chelsea soon finds romance with a Palestinian worker, Faraj, who has entered Israel from the Occupied Palestinian Territories without a legal work permit. This romance becomes a cause of tension with Chelsea's friends when Faraj, having lost employment, seeks refuge in their flat, hiding from the immigration police. Chelsea meets her tragic demise at the end of the musical when she is caught in a blast set off by a female suicide bomber while chasing after Faraj, who is fleeing from the police. The ending's multiple sensory and emotional pivots in quick succession require the audience to shift from shock to mourning and finally to delight. The emotional pivots enact the very emotional agility demanded of the migrant characters onstage, who face love, loss, dislocation, termination, and, many times, joy. The artistic maneuvers in the ending cover a range of sensorial registers around loss across the three renditions of Chelsea's death—one staged visually in narrative in Israel, the second aurally in darkness across different world cities, and last in an almost blindingly over-the-top finale onstage. The finale might challenge the viewer most in its demand to suspend mourning suddenly to celebrate and clap with the relocated survivors and the reanimated dead.

Rather than settling upon a redemptive and heroic finale, Maribel Legarda, the musical's director, insisted that "we did not want to give into the romance (of migratory life) knowing that death is random. As Pinoys, we move on. Not that we don't care, we have a controlled cry but not wallow because it's not just personal, it's about the community."[4] I interviewed Legarda and the playwright, Lisa Magtoto, during the first runs of the show in Manila to discuss the collaborative process behind their political and aesthetic choices. Both Legarda and Magtoto are longtime members of the Philippine Educational Theater Association (PETA), a politically progressive theater group founded in 1967. PETA premiered the high-energy musical in 2011, which saw its third run of shows in six months to sold-out audiences in Manila. PETA continued to produce the musical up to July 2017.

What is at stake in claiming a posture of not wallowing? Avoiding dramatic stasis, Legarda uses Chelsea's death as a catalyst to explore the generative, even multiplicative, potential of emotionalism in narratives of precarity. Rather than resort to pity or empathy for the condition of Filipino migrants in Israel or anywhere else in the world, Legarda offers another account for these emotional pivots:

> We *are* emotional, but we don't wallow. It isn't just personal; it's about the community. We don't wallow because we have a community that we can go to and talk to and cry with and laugh with. If you are migratory you are like that. If you have to leave, then . . . you find another community, and it just multiplies.[5]

To be emotional, then, is not simply a reflection of an interiority but a desire to connect with others. Wallowing is not a luxury afforded the audience or the individual characters in the musical, given the characters' emotional and economic labor, which is needed both by family back home and by employers in the host country. Rather than a catalyst for paralysis, crisis moments in the plot become moments of negotiation with a larger group: Faraj's entry into the Divas' community, Chelsea's employment termination, loss or lack of legal migrant status for others, or death. Mourning Chelsea's death in the end makes visible to friends or the audience the contours of a life lived. Emotions circulating among the members of the Diva collective are meant to make pain bearable, to be sure. However, more importantly, the display of emotions also makes more palpable the contours of the local community that gave shape to her life lived.

By definition, wallowing provides a comfort zone in sustaining an emotional state. To wallow in a situation is "to indulge in an unrestrained way in (something that creates a pleasurable sensation)."[6] Legarda's directorial decision responds to the Philippine media and government's rhetoric of describing overseas workers as *bagong bayani*, or "new national heroes," for the last four administrations up to the present one.[7] Her reaction criticizes the rhetoric of individual heroism and the attendant romantic nationalism proffered by the Philippine state. Simplifying the reasons for labor migration to some inherent nobility of character disavows the economic inequities at home that compel outmigration of skilled workers for export in the first place. This romanticization of labor naturalizes the difficult, sometimes tragic, conditions of the worker abroad for corporate marketing, in terms of a nation's comparative advantage, and for nationalist consumption at home. In this nationalist context, refusing to wallow mitigates a self-indulgent (nationalist) pleasure that forestalls more complicated narratives. Representing the story of the Filipino subject as an extension of the nation gets stuck in a conception of an unrecoverable past or a desire for a normative future. Not wallowing enables imagining other futures, conjuring other meanings for past events, and making manifest socialities that enable mutual or self-transformations.[8]

Affective refusal displaces and reframes narrative tropes and endings enforced by both origin and destination countries about the worker's experiences—a reframing that produces and recognizes socialities outside of nation-state demands. In one example of affective redirection, Martin Manalansan has described the posture of disaffection as necessary for survival among overseas Filipino workers. Disaffection for Manalansan means "not only emotional distance, alienation, antipathy, and isolation but also this word's other connotation of disloyalty to regimes of power and authority.... Disaffection emerges out of the need for survival and persistence in the midst of tribulations."[9] I would underscore that implied here is the migrant's relationship to "regimes of power and authority" represented by family and the Philippine brokerage nation-state. The hero narrative homogenizes all the personal and communal complexities, attachments, trials, joys, and deaths of migrant lives overseas into the self-same celebratory national romance. The light-filled finale casts literal light onto the audience, as if asking it to imagine non-national frames, including a queer and overindulgent present, to understand Chelsea's senseless death.

I read the capacity to shift moods, that is, to not wallow, not necessarily as an individuated experience but as a mode of *recognizing* and *creating* various socialities even in and alongside dominant narrative conditions. Not wallowing is a material affective response to unequal power, redirecting a relationship with a person, authority, or discourse so as to refuse to be in sync with that trajectory or timeline. Rather than view this refusal as agential heroism on the cheap or as an essential Filipino cultural trait, this affective agility is a response to the demands of continual suturing and keeping at bay multiple pressures of national histories and spaces that are not of one's own making. Not wallowing secures the ability to go from one situation to another, while recognizing how neoliberal disciplinary regimes demand labor flexibility through temporary contracts and economic precarity. The refusal to wallow that Legarda insists upon is therefore not just a defensive posture but also a productive one.

This artful shifting and display of emotion makes worlds sensible. I underscore Legarda's view of the inextricability of that affective stance from the subject's links to national, local, and informal communities as part of active world making. The art- and world-making capacity recalls the concept of *palabas*, a tactical manifestation of emotion discussed in the first chapter on *dating*. As Flores observed, "There is a deliberate agency at work in a gesture of performance or the process of making something appear and making it appear in a particular way (*papalabasin* or *pinapalabas*)."[10] While the circumstances may not necessarily be under one's control, *palabas* is agential insofar as how the revelation is made to appear in a specific context to a perceived audience, friend, family, stranger, and everything in between. The Philippine performance studies scholar Doreen Fernandez's work on *palabas* observes that performance is about the localized relationship between informed audience and performer.[11] Lucy San Pablo Burns extends Fernandez's insight to argue that this mutual acknowledgment of shared meanings in witnessing the "Filipina performing body under different forms and conditions of subjection" contains the archive of communal critique. Burns's conceptualization of "*puro arte*" makes evident the multiple functions of nonparodic performance.[12] As Legarda places the deployment of emotionalism at the fulcrum of the personal and the communal, emotions have material effects on making visible localized formations, whether between subjects or at each and every staged performance.

Affect is not simply its emotional manifestation as a codified endpoint. More importantly, it marks the process and conditions by which it is produced and its effects on its audience. The process generates audience, knowledge, and sociality and wields an affective and physical vocabulary shared by subject and receiver. Involving "acting, diversion, pedagogy," as Flores suggests, *palabas*, I would add, can be understood as a productive sociality in which performer and audience are engaged in reciprocal communication and transformation without the guarantee of a specific result but producing a sensible communality, a common sense, as Kandice Chuh has reconsidered. The performance renders visible the effects of state regulation of bodies and the technologies that create displaced and inassimilable subjects. Therefore, the "refusal to wallow"—the ability to switch modes and moods—would seem to regulate migratory life but always as a response to communal and material lived contexts.

Documenting Sensations of Invisibility

In May 2017, the *New York Times* drew attention for American readers to a well-known three-decade-old reality for Israelis and Filipinos, "Israel's Invisible Filipino Workforce," exploring the thriving cultural life of the forty thousand Filipino migrant workers in Israel.[13] Filipinos make up half the caregiver population of thirty thousand and are a large part of the hundred thousand foreign workers in Israel. In contemporary Israeli usage, the word for and body of the Filipino are synonymous with caregiver (*metapel*), who are most often ensconced in elderly people's homes or families six days a week and seen only in public accompanying an elderly citizen. The writer Ruth Margalit observes that "unlike other foreign workers, however, [Filipinos] are embedded deep within Israeli families, helping the most vulnerable members of society—or the most privileged." She writes that this "dual presence—transparent yet indispensable—discomfits the national imagination." Part of the discomfort is how this transparency shades onto the older Israeli citizen. Almost a decade earlier in 2008, the writer Ariel Hirschfeld published an editorial in *Haaretz*, a liberal Israeli English-language periodical, entitled "One Plus One Equals Zero," about a fictional older charge feeling invisible in Israeli society with "my Filipino."[14] The aggrieved figure describes himself as "one of the people with the Filipinos." He explains how "the moment we have a Filipino, no one sees us anymore."[15] The "Filipino" appears as a prosthetic to the citizen, now "doubled into a man plus another support-man" and ceasing to be part of the national optic. The presence of "my Filipino," the speaker claims, obscures the elderly citizen and blocks him from participating in the public sphere even as a respected member of it.[16] The speaker merges with the static "Filipino," the appendix that speaks, hears, moves, acts *for* the citizen, who himself remains unseen and unheard as "this zero of a-person-plus-a-Filipino": "With the Filipino you're signing off that it's the end for you."[17] Thus "the Filipino" marks not only the imminent end of the citizen's life but also the limit of belonging and political participation in the Israeli nation-state.

This unsettling feeling around Filipinos is rooted in a history of border closure and cultural consolidation of Israeli national identity. The process to create the invisible Filipino migrant as part of Israel's labor force began with moves to secure its internal borders as it strengthened its global relationships. The Filipino's invisible presence began in 1995, when Israel instituted Ha Tokhnit Ha Filipinit, or the Filipino Plan, to recruit Filipinos for geriatric care.[18] Under the Rabin Labor government (1992–1996), which initiated the expansion of global opportunities for Israel's economic growth, the Filipino Plan was approved two years after the border-closure policy against Palestinians in 1993—the material shoring up of Israeli borders. Supported by foreign investments and the private sector, these neoliberal policies came with the normalization of relations with Jordan after the first Oslo accords. Since then, the Filipino caregiver has become an indispensable member of Israeli family life but a dispensable worker for the Israeli state.

Haunting the troubling narrative about a foreign negation that negates the Israeli citizen is another figure that also marks the limits of belonging in Israel, the Palestinian. As Rebecca Stein points out in *Itineraries of Conflict*, the Rabin era also put in motion representational practices in film production and tourism development to shore up the intelligibility of Israeli borders by making such Israeli cultural representation Palestinian-free.[19] These policies effectively delineated state and private borders against undesirable internal migrations, namely, Palestinians, in material and representational terms. To note, Filipinos did *not* replace Palestinians as caregivers, but Filipinos were part of a plan to privatize geriatric care, save the state money, and also consolidate and secure family borders by making these borders manageable via legal and timed deportation. Along with other temporary migrants—Thai, Chinese, Russian, and Nepalese—who filled specific occupational niches in construction, agriculture, and transportation, they would be allowed to stay for a maximum of five years, after which the visa held by the employer would expire. Since non-Jewish migrants are not covered by the "right of return," these Filipino caregivers cannot make *aliyah*, a religious act of migration into Israel, and are therefore ineligible for Israeli citizenship. Immediately deportable upon loss of their employment or death of the employer,[20] the caregiver's presence in the Israeli nation-state depends on maintaining economic and affective relations within Israeli homes. The invisibility of the Filipino caregiver and the Israeli charge as expressed in the *Haaretz* editorial made a second order of cultural invisibility possible: the managed inequality around racialized internal and external borders.

Disappeared into Love

Against this backdrop of intimacy with an invisible yet troubling population, Tomer Heymann made his moving documentary film *Paper Dolls (Bubot Niyar)*, originally a three-hour, six-episode miniseries on Israeli television before being edited to eighty-five minutes for the Berlin Film Festival in 2006. The documentary followed five of the Dolls— Salvador "Sally" Comatoy, Chiqui Diokno, Giorgio Diokno, Troan Jacob "Jan" Libas, and Francisco "Cheska" P. Ortiz Jr.—through their stories of caring for elderly Orthodox men, romance, and eventually the spate of bombings and immigrant police raids that resulted in the detention, deportation, and eventual emigration of the film's subjects. The film provided a primer for an Israeli television and later international film audience on the lives of queer and racially marked temporary workers that many citizens did not see or chose not to see yet who were a ubiquitous presence in many families and neighborhoods. In the opening scene, the camera enters the small clubs frequented by migrant workers around the Central Bus Station in Tel Aviv, a gritty neighborhood where many foreign workers live and play. In one of the smaller clubs, Heymann encounters Sally and the other Filipino caregivers known as the drag act Paper Dolls. Onstage as the Dolls, the subjects take turns lip-synching as glamorous divas or as backup singers in matching outfits. Sometimes the Dolls would wear intricate evening gowns made from old newspapers, resplendently tailored for their transformed bodies. The campiness of discarded newspapers repurposed into beautiful vestments projected mock-glamour but also suggested the donning of the national imaginary of the Israeli newspapers.[21] Newspapers are one-day bestsellers, after all, as Benedict Anderson observed of national print culture.[22] The national castoffs imprinted, adorned, and enfolded the performing migrant bodies with the sediment of yesterday's news, signaling their fleeting ephemerality and dispensability in the national community. Being attired in this costume for the evening also acknowledged this possession of a national past-time as temporary as the Dolls themselves.

In documenting the Dolls' performance, the film captured moments almost epic as Heymann framed the Filipino bodies in slow motion onstage. Often, the documentary presented the Dolls' staged performances without the actual song they were lip-synching to. While the sonic omission was in part a practical choice involving intellectual property rights, the result produced important aesthetic effects. The texture of the moving bodies separate from the mimicked referent becomes the focus. This scopic/sonic split in the film editing emphasized the texture of the Dolls' performing bodies by taking away one level of artificiality, the voice of another performance. In its place was the Dolls' and also the filmmaker's artifice. The bodies as bearers of mimicry and of time through the slow motion were not removed so immediately as to become another body or voice but provided the clarity of surfaces as open possibilities. Thus these sequences indexed but did not seal the citational interpellation by an ideal discourse, leaving only the Dolls' bodies and their movement in time—bodies in the process of imitating and projecting for an audience. The sonic/scopic split operated to open multiple levels of meaning making for the Dolls and the film, to put in question attempts to close the circuit of narrative through love and authenticity, a circuit the rest of the film took pains to show.

Choosing lip-synching drag performers to serve as the film's argument for workers' right to live in Israel posed a particular challenge for Heymann. The very desire to make his Filipino friends and subjects visible and deserving meant synchronizing them into normative family and national time. In its quest to align with the genuine and authentic, the documentary therefore highlighted the heartwarming and compelling relationship between Haim, an Israeli bronchial cancer survivor, and Sally/Salvador, his Filipino caregiver. When Haim was eighty-two, his family requested a male caregiver, and Sally/Salvador came into his life to cook, clean, and care for him. Genuine affection bonded them, one attending the end of life of the other. At one point, Sally even suggests that she and Haim celebrate their upcoming fortieth and ninetieth birthdays together; the touching scene is followed by a cut to Haim's funeral, where she walks last in the procession behind the family. Names of mourning relatives are invoked in the background, while a heart-wrenching close-up on Sally's face captures tears, physical signs of interior truth, as she weeps by a nearby gravesite. In the end, she remains unnamed in the litany of loved ones.

Sally's figuration as caring mother *and* surrogate daughter of Israel at once was multiply bound by a national performance of language, of proper gender roles, and of reciprocal and "authentic" love, seemingly apart from economic relations. The film took pains to produce and deploy the visuality of Sally's body as a feminine-presenting one. Of the five at the time of filming, only Sally, who had taken hormones to reshape her body, was shown with her shoulder-length hair down and dressed in short shorts and spaghetti-strap tops.[23] The others dressed only on weekends and were otherwise shown in gender-neutral clothing with hair tied back for work. When interviewed, Sally was usually shot inside the house, thus domesticating her voice further. Sally's near-fluency in Hebrew and her willingness to be taught to read Hebrew poetry and learn Jewish culture were striking for an Israeli viewer. For Diaspora Jews who choose to immigrate and settle in Israel, the learning of modern Hebrew as the unifying language of the Diaspora is a sign of the true commitment to Israeli society, and for Sally, to Haim.[24] Interestingly, Sally also served as Haim's voice, reading his notes and interpreting for him on the phone, as he had limited speaking ability. As Sally would lend Haim her voice when he could not speak, Haim in turn offered her a language and culture of national belonging. In another scene, Sally reads the poem of Yehuda Amichai, a renowned Israeli literary figure, under Haim's tutelage, about reciprocal support: "Sometimes I lean on the handle of the wheelchair in which I push them." The gendered, classed, and tutelary intimacy brokers the intimacy between Sally as migrant worker and the Israeli and international audience. Sally's figuration as surrogate child enacts a "racialization of intimacy," in David Eng's term, in the ever-receding visibility of race and racism to render the Filipino caregiver assimilable (but ultimately dispensable) and, most importantly, to produce the affective wall that would make visible the outlines of a benevolent Israeli nation-state.[25]

For the figure of Sally to achieve such acceptance, her lip-synch must go beyond the stage into the realm of work: She is made to speak as a substitute daughter in order to draw out the film's argument for the care worker's social, cultural, and familial belonging. As Flores asserted, *palabas* "is a matter of conjuring, tricking the eye, catching the feeling, concealing the device of drama. And because it is tactical, it is also corruptive: semblance is always elusive." Posing as another person onstage could lead to suspicions about posing as a caregiver for the elderly at home or, worse, posing as a legitimate subject of the state. Poised between belonging to a host family yet not belonging to the nation-state, the Filipino caregivers as performers represent a discomfiting figure, finding tenuous resolution in an appeal to melodramatic, familial emotionalism. As with the newspaper gowns, her transformation through migration and costuming depend entirely on the protective layers that the host nation-state provisionally allows and that she must take on. Yet even in the heartwarming tutelary scene are moments of Sally misreading the poem about care, duty, and subservience, giving lie to the fact that assimilation and submission, even at its enunciation, could ever be satisfactory. When the voice to be mimicked is turned off, the film audience views only the bodies in the process of mimicking—whether gender, care, love, or filiality—the very categories diffracted in the club space but managed strictly beyond it.

Family Is a Nightmare

By deliberate contrast to *Paper Dolls*, in *Care Divas* family is a living nightmare. While the documentary depicted a seamless synchrony of the modern Israeli state with family sentimentalism, the musical keeps in view the vexed relationships with and among the overlapping national borders of Palestine, Israel, and the Philippines and the varying gender, race, and labor formations that each imbrication brings. For Shai as the foil to Chelsea, the Philippines is manifest in a mother figure who, rather than a limitless font of love, intermittently haunts and terrifies him. Throughout the musical, the nightmare Filipino parent is lip-synched by the older Israeli charge or one or more of the other characters, underscoring the multiple psychic landscapes the migrant inhabits all at once. Lights dim, and the possessed actor is lit from below to create an eerie and grotesque image onstage. Haunting does not denote an afterlife but an ever-present condition whereby other places and other times simultaneously demand the migrant's attention. Lip-synching, the provenance of the performers, is put to different use in these haunting scenes. The body possessed by another from another place interrupts the narrative to convey psychic violence and imprisonment, not pleasure.

Shai:
Nakakarindi na ang boses mong naririnig
Maya't-maya ako'y binubugbog ng iyong bibig
Buhay ka pa pero ako'y minumulto mo na
Pumipitik sa bawat kong kibot nagpapaalala.

Ang bawat kilos ko'y de susi't may nagbabantay
Ang buhay ko ang hawak-hawak ng ibang kamay
Nabanat na
Konting hatak pa'y mapipigtas na siya
Kailangan kong kumawala Kailangan ko na.
Sinasakal aking pulso hindi makahinga
Tumakas sa isang kulungan
Para lang lumipat sa isang bagong kulungan
Naku, naku, naku
Ano pa ba'ng pwedeng mangyari dito?
Parang wala na.
Parang wala na.

[How cloying your voice,
Every second it berates and beats me.
You're alive, but you haunt me still,
Taunting my every move and making your presence felt.
Each move I make there's a guard with a key.
My life is controlled by another's hands,
Beaten and stretched.
One more tug and I'll come undone.
I need to get away, I really need to get away
I'm choking and can't breathe.
I fled one prison
To go to another.
My oh my
What can happen here?
Nothing it seems.
Nothing at all.][26]

The song as musical monologue extends a moment in which Shai can express the feeling of stuckness, where "nothing" happens in both host and origin country, "Nothing it seems / Nothing at all," given labor demands. Spaces haunting other spaces in the present show the affective overlap of synchronic national times. As Bliss Lim has astutely pointed out in terms of monsters and ghosts, "the fantastic unsettles the fantasy of a single calendrical present shared by all citizens through an *occult splintering of the national meanwhile*."[27] The present is overfull and contains multiple times and locations at once. Refuge, freedom, or self-realization is found neither in the Philippines nor Israel, as both places constrain Shai, making burdensome bodily and psychic demands: "Beaten and stretched / one more tug and I'll come undone." The irony of the present (instead of the past) and the living (instead of the dead) haunting Shai indicates how other spaces provide sources of fantasies and nightmares that pull him in different psychic directions.

Migration is not an escape from the economic and emotional demands of family but instead a mode of internalizing these multiple demands. Simply beside himself, from both fright and anxiety, Shai is unable to achieve self-integration given the pulls in different directions by family employers and family at home. At the root of his feeling of stasis is the compulsion to embody others' physical or economic needs to the negation of his own desires. For Shai, the concept of family returns to its roots as a functional and proprietary concept. Engels would remind the reader in *The Origin of Family, Private Property, and the State* that

> the original meaning of the word "family" (*familia*) is not that compound of sentimentality and domestic strife which forms the ideal of the present-day philistine; among the Romans it did not at first refer to the married pair and their children, but only to slaves.

He goes on to quote Marx:

> The modern family contains in germ not only slavery (*servitus*), but also serfdom, since from the beginning it is related to agricultural services. It contains *in miniature* all the contradictions which later extend throughout society and its state.[28]

With this reminder of labor and power built into the concept of family, the haunting parent reflects the family concept as always already haunted by this exploitative relation. Being possessed shades too easily into being a possession as coerced labor. *Care Divas* complicates the intimacy the documentary naturalizes between parent and child by highlighting the emotionally oppressive call of family duty and obligation. These dovetail with the labor exploitation that is elided in both nation-states when framed at the level of family intimacy. For Shai, death is not stasis; rather, to be continually haunted by others' needs is the cause of emotional eruptions and disruptions.

Privileging hetero-reproduction in service of racial capital,[29] the fantastical attachment to nation as a natural extension of family produces sentimental seamlessness. *Care Divas* questions this attachment, given "all the contradictions which later extend throughout society and its state," as Engels reveals. Shai's character illustrates how ties to the biological family in this global frame are riven with emotional coercion, similar to what Angel experiences in Diaz's documentary. Like Angel, Shai not having children is seen as lacking, if not refusing, responsibilities and justifies why he should send his family more of his earnings: "Malaki na-man ang sweldo mo. Wala ka namang pinag-iipunang anak" ("You earn so much! And you don't have children to save for!"). Shai responds, "You, you are my child." To be a nonreproductive homosexual (or any orienta-tion, for that matter) is to have no responsibility for a future. To be ho-mosexual is to be already excessive, unproductive, and useless. By this logic, if one cannot recreate such a community through reproduction, then the condition of belonging is to support the family and kin that can do so. Refusing this obligation effectively cancels filial membership. The queer subject's frustration and rejection of this logic in the musical de-naturalize such an attachment, based on heteronormative expectations. "Queer subcultures," Halberstam suggests, "produce alternative tempo-ralities by allowing their participants to believe that their futures can be imagined according to the logics that lie outside of the paradigmatic markers of life experience—namely, birth, marriage, reproduction, and death."[30] The refusal to participate in such heterosexual life markers ex-cludes the queer subject such as Shai from family and national futures but also necessitates imagining "alternative temporalities." The space to imagine the forms of queer time and place Halberstam suggests is mani-fest in two instances in the musical: Chelsea's fatal romance with a Pal-estinian worker and the Divas' performance space. Both these plot elements instantiate interruptions in narrative expectations to explore fleeting bonds of intimacy.

Stupidity of Love

While Shai depicts the overwrought and oppressive nature of two nation-states that deploy family sentiment to mask economic exploitation, Chelsea's situation complicates this further when she forms an unsanc-tioned relationship with Faraj, a Palestinian. The queer erotic-romantic relationship between Faraj and the feminine-presenting Chelsea problem-atizes the attachment to nation. Chelsea, the foreign migrant, is torn be-tween adoptive family loyalty in the figure of his employer Isaac and erotic love in the figure of Faraj. This latter intimacy explored by the Chelsea character is not present in the documentary but also reveals national sub-ject positions that are historically incommensurate. Chelsea, the Filipino guest worker, must grapple with the multiple claims over home, nation, and belonging between Palestinians and Israelis. Chelsea's place in Israel is secured by Isaac being alive and is clearly fortified by her filial duty toward the contractual employer and to her family back in the Philip-pines. Once Isaac dies, however, her place in Israel is no longer secure, and her days in Israel are numbered. Her tie with the nation-state depends solely on her economic tie to her employer, not necessarily her emotional one. On the other hand, Faraj symbolizes another source of fulfillment, one independent of family duty and economic demand. However, the Israeli-Palestinian conflict makes the romance impossible, or at least short-lived, as both are immediately deportable and expendable under Israeli law.

The Middle East conflict is not lost on Magtoto and Legarda and is re-staged when tensions flare regarding the negotiation of shared domestic space. Faraj later seeks refuge in Chelsea's and the other caregivers' home after he loses his job. Having entered Israel from the Territories with a false identity and without a work permit, he cannot safely go back home. During his stay, Chelsea's housemates demand that Faraj conform to the rules of the house. Chelsea quickly reminds them that all Faraj's life he has been forced to conform to other people's rules. The migrants do not fully belong in Israel either, since their residency expires with their con-tracts. Some of the caregivers share with Faraj the status of being "ille-gal," having been fired or having lost employment upon the employer's death. Thus "overstaying" is a precarious state shared by Faraj in the Divas' home and by some of the Divas in Israel. However, Chelsea points out that the caregivers are paid to conform to Israeli law and custom, while Faraj's terms of belonging in Israel as a Palestinian is a custodial, colo-nized one. As technologies of state exclusions, illegality and criminality converge through distinct but now linked histories in both Filipino and Palestinian subjects, whose mobility and presence are contained by the laws of the Israeli nation-state. Addressing issues of migration, coloniza-tion, dislocation, homelessness, criminalization, and violence, Magtoto and Legarda gesture to the different historical trajectories of settler colo-nialism and migrant precarity that lend and nuance a shared vocabulary between the subjects of each.

Immigration and expired visas among foreign workers were not seen as a threat in Israel until after the second intifada in 2000. The Special Immigration police was formed around 2002 to ferret out overstaying, therefore illegal, immigrants in Israel. Those who were once invited guest workers could easily and often become lawbreakers subject for deporta-tion. The preservation of the national character, national security, and economic expansion colluded to make possible in the popular and state imagination the connection between Filipinos as domesticated aliens and Palestinians as internal aliens. This legal and affective complication has a return effect on the Filipino worker: The Filipino becomes a potential target for the violent xenophobia visited upon Israel's internal aliens. The desirable substitute converges with the undesirable displaced object. Since the foreign caregiver is at once part of the extended family and a national outsider, at a time of extreme border policing this position makes her an ambivalent figure that can shift easily from invited guest to foreign threat. In the context of refugees and border crossers in the United Kingdom, Sara Ahmed has described how very different alien figures can be connected in state-sponsored paranoia:

> The slide between figures constructs a relation of resemblance between figures: what makes them alike may be their "unlikeness" from "us." Within the narrative hate cannot be found in one figure but works to create the very outline of different figures or objects of hate, a creation that crucially aligns the figures together and constitutes them as a "common" threat. . . . Hate is economic; it circulates between signifiers in relationships of difference and displacement.[31]

Xenophobic affect is able to stick from one body to another, though the bodies might have varying histories and relationships to the state. Thus, foreign caregiver and colonized subject both cast out from the national family remain under state custody.

Chelsea and Faraj have to be contained by the Israeli nation-state as members of subgroups who do not share in national historical time, exposing the ideological labor necessary to shore up continually overlapping and incommensurate borders of family and home to produce national historical time. This shoring up necessitates the management of affective life mired in the complex violence involved in managing racial, religious, sexual, and political borders and territory. Rather than romantic internationalism, the musical illustrates how the migrant situation continually rubs up against other precarious histories and conflicts, thus expanding the scope of the political sensorium and suggesting what labor and migratory politics might mean for each locale. Radically different colonial histories and spaces nuance key political terms such as "labor," "home," "displacement," and "disenfranchisement." The distance of the Middle East locale is made familiar through this sedimentation articulated in the musical as comparative material historical conditions for the migrant and colonized characters.

The affective life of living along interstitial spaces where borders continually enfold, break, shift, fall away, and overlap does not follow smooth narrative endings, as in the case of Chelsea's death. Given that Chelsea's (and arguably Faraj's) life is conditioned by multiple national histories and demands, the notion of a neat romantic ending fails to capture the com-

plexity of narrative unfolding. When Faraj flees from the immigration police, the musical chorus portends Chelsea's imminent death.

Song: "Pinili Niyang Maging Tanga"
Pinili niyang maging tanga
Sa ngalan ng pag-ibig pinili niya . . .

[He chose to be stupid.
In the name of love, he chose to be stupid . . .]

The chorus fades on an extended and suspended open vowel in the word
tanga (stupid), displaced by a choral sigh. While seemingly dismissive,
to diminish Chelsea's choice to empty "stupidity" is to question the very
conditions of choosing itself while resisting the easy and trite conclusion
that Chelsea "died for love." Thus, romance and its explanatory power are
also refused.

Contingency, disruptions, eruptions, accident, and context determine
the limits of agency, which itself does not offer romantic closure. However, according to the lyrics, the excesses of love result in Chelsea's death,
defying easy economic and family logics. To refuse these logics is to refuse the easy aesthetic closure that national heroism or normative love
pairings offers. What on the surface blames the victim evinces in the song
a deeper lament and anger over Chelsea and the circumstances of her
death in a historical conflict. Yet the content of the song returns events
leading to her death back to Chelsea as a complicit agent in the history of
this conflict who "chose to be stupid." That is, she chose the inappropri-
ate (according to the employing nation-state) love object over the economic demands of loyalty to her Philippine family or Israeli employer. If
stupidity displaces and signals the limit of capitalist love, the narrative is
left with actors and indeterminate endings that lead to death without
meaning. This disallows heroism itself, since heroes are not supposed to
die meaningless deaths, even if meaning has to be imbued retroactively.
Both individual love and national heroism provide an aesthetic frame to
death. In this case, anger works alongside pity and sadness to inform the
musical's refusal to wallow in either scenario. The song denies individual or national love as a reason for her death, so that love and death are
not easily conjoined without interrogation of power itself.

The protagonist's untimely death figures as timely friction that over-
flows sensorially and exceeds the logics of national, gender, sexual, and
racial histories that fail to capture the sense of her life and death. Chelsea's death stands, as she does in the end, squarely at the intersection of
pleasure and pain, romantic and economic intimacies, nationalism and

violent anticolonial resistance, and state policing of internal and external borders. Indeed, Chelsea's love and death are casualties of a longer history of Palestinian struggle against a colonial structure. The musical challenges expectations around domestic and national dramas to make visible the imbricated borders of Israel, Palestine, and the Philippines, produced, broken down, then reproduced and negotiated as part of the workers' everyday experience. In linking together the fates of these dispensable and colonized marginalized subjects, the musical expands and complicates the political sensorium around Filipino migrants and migrancy shaped by frictive histories of racializations and various nation-building projects.[32]

Conjuring Community

One of the opening numbers in *Care Divas* frames the two worlds occupied by the characters: On the one hand, the migrants serve as labor and income source, and on the other, at night, they escape to the stage with the audience and other performers in order to secure a presence in a self-created fantasy world. Emerging from their invisibility as abstracted affective labor for the Israeli family and income source for the Philippine family, they escape to center stage at night to "bloom" among other migrant workers:

Lahat:
Mabuti na lang at may kaibigan na laging matatakbuhan
Ang aming lipstick at ang wig at ang may sequins na gown
Sa piling nila ay mag-iinit muli
Ang nanlalamig naming kaluluwa!
Iwanan sandali ang orinola't suwero
At tanganang mahigpit ang matabang mikropono
Ibubuka'ng bibig, bibirit ng notang nasa tono.
Tulad ng mga ligaw na bulaklak Ihagis man sa putik . . . Kami'y
    mamumukadkad
Sa inyong palakpak at halik . . .

[ALL:
Good thing there are friends I can run to.
Our lipstick, wig, and sequined gowns
Against my skin
Warm my cold, lifeless soul.
Leave my bedpan and medicines,
Grab the thick microphone

Open my mouth wide and hit that note.
Like stray flowers, cast out in the mud,
We will bloom
With your kisses and applause.]

Transformed by the make up, wigs, and sequined gowns, the migrant's bodies are put to other, more pleasurable uses. Onstage, these "OFW princesses," OFW (Overseas Filipino Workers) being a Philippine state designation for the emigrants, walk the tenuous line between fantasy and reality to make the everyday bearable. The lyrics shift from pondering the drudgery of work to sexualized titillation and pleasure. The act of singing with the "thick" microphone is described in sexual terms. The phrase "to hit that note" plays on the double meaning of *nota* in Filipino gay lingo as both musical note and male genitalia. While winking at the theater audience with this wordplay, the performer takes pleasure in hitting the heights of intense pleasure in the musical and sexual feat for the diegetic audience. The lyrics' play on words, using metaphors of bodily transformation, and the physical transformation create moments of pleasure for the audience, narrative audience, and performer in their double role as caregivers and care divas. As Burns points out, the "re-creation/recreation is an active and playful consumption of hegemonic standards of beauty, femininity, and masculinity that are corrupted, transformed, and pleasured through the act of performance."[33] This staged moment of fusion of the two roles transforms the act of care away from the original economic forces and directed for the pleasure of the diegetic audience composed of other migrants and for the Filipino audience. Queer bodies, rendered unreproductive and useless for some, generate new meanings and temporalities onstage. In their nonutilitarian hypervisibility as performers, care as a form of labor in their stage performance is no longer bound solely to market exchange but channeled to other modes of affective relations that reveal outlines of another space and time of (queer and displaced) communities.

The Care Divas' hypervisibility onstage is a performance of precarity that cites their invisibility as domestic labor in Israel and their physical displacement as export labor from the Philippines. As Judith Butler observes in the case of undocumented workers singing the national anthem in Spanish in public, "[the singing] exposes the modes of disavowal through which the nation constitutes itself. In other words, the singing exposes and opposes those modes of exclusion through which the nation imagines and enforces its own unity."[34] The recreational space becomes a site of shared meanings (with diegetic and actual audience) and critique of nation-state as a self-aware group. Reassessing the role of the drag queen troupe in *Paper Dolls* the documentary, Manalansan has argued that

> [the subjects] are performing a "care of the self" as Foucault terms it. In "care of the self," Foucault argues for the ways in which the subject "cultivates" or more appropriately "labors" to constitute a sense of self through quotidian activities. This process of self-cultivation is in many ways disciplined and constrained, while at the same time it is also a space where the subject may feel a sense of exuberant freedom.[35]

In the comical and pleasurable moment of the double entendre and linguistic play, I would add that the "self-cultivation" and "exuberant freedom" that Manalansan signals in the stage performance is also at once the moment of communal (trans)formation. "We will bloom with your kisses and applause" recognizes the role that the narrative audience (and by extension the theater audience) plays to effect this care of self. The diva persona (brought about by the wigs and sequined gowns) and audience approbation are inextricable elements that possess the performer. The audience is transformed and transported with the performer. Thus the spectacle is the reflection of communal affect. As with the fan video in the Introduction and Dorotea's karaoke rendition in Chapter 1, adulation, here in the form of "applause and kisses," is valuation that serves as reciprocal care and social accumulation without profit. The dressing and performing underscore the communality of this version of care and "self-cultivation." While fleeting, these moments of care remain outside the purview of either nation-state and privatized at the expense of the migrant, as a defense against the disquieting effects of family demands in both host and origin countries.

Rather than see the lip-synch act in the small Filipino and migrant clubs in both *Care Divas* and *Paper Dolls* as simply an outlet from and adjustment to the drudgery of work conditions, the stage act might be read as a different "labor of love"—a type of caregiving for the migrant community and the creation of *biyuti* as personhood, to use Martin Manalansan's term.[36] In her work in the Bicol region of the Philippines, and in line with Southeast Asian notions of beauty, the anthropologist Fenella Cannell has described the place of the *bakla*: "The *bakla* epitomize these recapturings of power, not literally through possession, but through a wrapping of the body in symbols of protective status, and a transformation of the persona by proximity to the power it imitates, which are in many ways akin to it."[37] Such recapturing and possession of power acknowledges this possession as temporary, but this status is achieved through effort and labor. This labor of self-fashioning is *not* recognized or funded by either the Philippine or the Israeli state. The act acknowledges shared material lack within and across migrant communities, the economic lack in the Philippines, their marginal or undocumented status in Israel, and their varied absence in both national spaces. This camp performance of excess to underscore the many types of lack is what delights their Filipino audience-admirers. The *biyuti*/beauty of the performers emerges only in this reciprocal and mutual acknowledgment.

Given this reciprocity, the lip-synch performance is a type of care that is not a commodity, that is, something for which labor is extracted as surplus value. As the Dolls transform on stage, in that moment other migrant workers reorient their own bodies differently and take part in the fleeting bond between performer and viewer. Cannell's description of beauty contests, a mainstay of island and overseas Filipino community celebrations, connects beauty and personhood.

> The dual kinds of "beauty" to which the contestants here staking claim [are] on the one hand, personal prettiness . . . and on the other, those aspects of "beauty" which can be bought—grand clothes, complete make-up, the evidence of who is behind you, and the affirmative acclamation of the crowd.[38]

Thus, *biyuti* as personhood beyond personal appearance comes to light only in communality with the evidence of audience support and acclamation. The staged performance may then be understood as a form of address that generates a community at the same that it generates pleasure and critique. The rehearsal and performance spaces in the Filipino community provide a form of glamorous hypervisibility and become supplemental sites of care that countered the Dolls' and other Filipinos' abject invisibility as professional caregivers in Israel and as absent providers for families in the Philippines. The Dolls create nonutilitarian uses for their serviceable bodies outside of proscribed national and family narratives that would transform them from workers to persons. This immaterial labor from "deliberate agency" circulates to create the terms of the local Filipino community and its self-legibility, outside of state and reproductive family dictates but conditioned by them. Outside the "empire of care" in which the intimacy between employer and employed is assumed is a communality of care directed away from imperial and market dictates.[39] The transformation is projected not toward an "end" but rather to an event that could be repeated over and again across and beyond national spaces and times.

Coda

On a crisp day in 2010 in London, where the documentary *Paper Dolls* was enjoying another run, I spoke with Chiqui, one of the original Dolls, who some years back had emigrated to the United Kingdom to become a head nurse. Israel had proven inhospitable as a long-term destination and could not take him as a permanent resident. In particular, I asked him about the difference between performing for a local migrant Filipino audience and an Israeli audience. Chiqui responded, "Well, with an Israeli audience they just dance and they don't care; with Filipinos you expect them to do what Filipinos always do: They reach out and hug and almost kiss you. You feel like a star. . . . When I perform I make myself happy; I forget my troubles, and I make the other Filipinos forget, too, and be happy."[40] Since the group formed in 1998, the pre- and postperformance community of the Dolls and the migrant Filipino audience that loved them together carved out a space and time of pleasure and beauty outside of their expected roles as financial providers for families in the Philippines and emotional providers in Israeli homes.[41] Making other Filipinos forget, as Chiqui described, their unflagging duty to either Philippine or Israeli national fantasy opens other possibilities to share space with others.

The lyrics and plotline of *Care Divas* thematize the effects of these simultaneous transnational intersections across time and place. The overlay of the Israeli-Palestinian conflict *with* and alongside the migrant condition but distinguishing these sociohistorical conditions is brought to Filipinos in the musical and dramatized for Filipinos in Manila through the lens and experience of queer subjects living this global history. This show about migrants and homes facilitates the expansion of a political sensorium between host and home countries, bringing global and regional politics into queer spaces, times, and communalities. As Gonzalves and Burns point out, performing a play does not only provide diversion; it also offers the "chance to encounter the past in a corporeal fashion" and "to call the community into being."[42] The applause and light-filled finale in *Care Divas* performs such a transformative call to make legible queer and precarious connections, bringing the theatrical audience into the impossibility outside of time. The sensorial experience gives shape to this fleeting communality in the musical's virtual time and place, indexing an impossible time and place in dialogue with other elsewheres.

Coda: Presence and Mourning to the Future

Ten thousand miles and twelve hours apart, the siblings texted back and forth in real time. I sat beside my friend George as he watched the wake in the morning from his computer screen in my apartment. As we watched, he sent a text to his sister onscreen at the Manila funeral parlor, St. Peter, where it is evening, to ask who the man sitting in the back is. The man looked incredibly like their father, who had just passed away. She texted back that he was an uncle from the provinces that he had not seen before. The camera was a bit blurry, and I wondered if the problem was my internet connection or Manila's. The reception was choppy, and the images often lagged a bit. In one half-second the sister was sitting down; the next half-second, she was headed to greet a guest. The coffin was in the foreground. The seating area, wooden pews, was in the upper right of the screen. The guests gathered, and a prayer service was to be offered sometime in the next hour. The live-streaming of the wake, or *e-burol*, was a video service offered by the funeral home chain in the Philippines. *Burol* is Tagalog for wake, and the popularized e- prefix denotes it is taking place in the clouds, not the religious but the virtual kind, that is, cyberspace. Given the dispersal of Filipinos around the world, this has become common practice to connect families on these important and solemn occasions.

Amid the global pandemic in 2020, daily and significant ritual human encounters had to go online. In early April, with tens of thousands dead from the disease in the United States, a touching piece in the *New York Times*, "The Surprising Intimacy of the Live-Streamed Funeral," brought attention to the recent necessity of live-streaming funerals here in the

United States.[1] After international border closures, a Canadian resident could not attend her aunt's funeral in Los Angeles. The family decided upon a small service to be live-streamed for those unable to travel. The same week, the *Boston Globe* told of a moving memorial on Zoom for a thirty-one-year-old Boston resident set up by the young man's older brother for family and friends in Alabama and elsewhere.[2] The mourners dressed, prepared pictures and slides of the young man, and stayed to drink and chat after the memorial. While not a common practice before the pandemic in most communities, these remote practices have become a necessity for many families faced with social distancing and limited travel during the height of the health crisis, in which many died alone. Only about 20 percent of funeral homes in the United States offered this service as of 2019.[3] The live-streaming is usually for the actual memorial service.

Vigils in the Philippines, however, are twenty-four-hour affairs that last a week, with family members always present in the room. For many in communities whose families are dispersed around the globe, versions of remote grieving have been an indispensable mainstay for years, often deploying text threads, 4G technology, and phone cameras to join loved ones in different time zones. I look at this mediated mourning practice common in and made necessary by Filipino diasporic life to explore various embodied conceptions of sociality and relationality when time and space do not coincide but are juxtaposed through a mediated interface.[4] Digital mourning is a twenty-first-century way to deploy and deal with the same long-distance networks of both people and technology that global capital has put in place. *E-burol* as a service is a technological affordance that sutures the disruptions in Filipino lives wrought by nation-state laws and borders as well as the economic imperatives for migration from global South to North. Across the globe, Skype, Facebook, FaceTime, Viber, and other interface services are normalized options to maintain contact with loved ones for middle- and working-class families who depend on remittance income.[5] Filipino families use these communications media to meet status obligations and maintain personal ties. In this synchrony of mourning, for a predominantly Catholic country where viewing the dead is an important part of the funerary ritual, *e-burol* is a way for those far away to be present at funerals when they cannot physically attend, usually because of the prohibitive costs of airfare, their job schedule, or legal precarities that do not permit such easy movement.[6]

Since the medium affords entry and exit into various modes of time—ritual time, everyday time, and end times, *e-burol* makes manifest various ways of being with others. I highlight two Tagalog concept-words here that map other ways to generate ecologies of communality. My use of ecology marks not just the actual nodes of connectivity but the interrelationships and flows among people, places, affects, and meanings, to shift focus away from the enabling boundary and onto the various ways of being with others who are familiar but may not completely share time and place. The first, *pakiramdam* (literally, to make oneself felt, or to feel a presence), is affective engagement without immediate proximity at all. This may result from an act as direct as a visit, an email, a phone call, or a letter, or it can be as indirect and vague as being told of a sighting or to spot someone passing on the street. In all cases, the feeling, rather than act, acknowledges the presence and one's affinity with another. *Pakiramdam* can as easily refer to an engagement with spirits and nonhuman entities and even with ideas, abstraction, and situations. That is, one could feel one's way around or grapple with an object or idea. The second, *kapiling*, with the collectivizing *ka-* prefix, is to be in someone's proximity or vicinity but does not necessarily include or demand any interaction between the two parties. One can be in the same room without necessarily engaging with the other or communicating as a point of contact. This relationality registers how a person's proximity generates connectivity without direct interaction. Both *pakiramdam* and *kapiling* recognize that two or more parties, who might have a passing or previous history, are engaged in generating a shared but fluid relationship. ˉ

E-burol, or live-streamed vigils, sets these ecologies of communality in motion in fraught but productive ways. The distance *and* proximity the medium facilitates mitigates and modulates the intensity of feeling by allowing the one abroad to adjust degrees of participation and communality. *E-burol* is not simply a digital reincorporation of the family in real time, though that is an effect given the cultural force of the category. However, the various modes of mourning also reveal, I would underscore, other notions of being with others in shared communality. The practice of digital mourning indexes, as in the sites I explored in the previous chapters, the simultaneous and multiple affective labor transpiring in different locations for different ends, service wages abroad and sustaining social ecology at home. Furthermore, technology, as in the corporate offshore site and used by teachers and caregivers, expands the present through these spatial juxtapositions. Therefore it makes possible the modulation of being present with and to others—visual, physical, and virtual, to name a few. Digital mourning as a form of communing generates an atmosphere that transforms "here" and "there" into a shared interval with others and acknowledges the multiple rhythms that comprise the present for each subject. Thus, this imperfect medium registers how living labor in the face of death enables various ways to be present amid incommensurable strands and rhythms of different lives at once.

Pakiramdam: Visuality without Visibility

St. Peter Chapels bills itself as "Death Care experts," with twenty-three megachapels and many smaller ones throughout Manila and other sizeable cities across the archipelago. Founded in 1975 a few years after the Marcos government inaugurated the *balikbayan* program, St. Peter Chapels claims to have "continuously led the memorial services industry through pioneering technological innovations like the St. Peter E-Burol, St. Peter E-Libing and St. Peter Tribute."[7] While *e-burol* live-streams the wake in closed circuit, "e-libing" streams the actual burial or cremation service, and the "tribute" is an online site designed for each deceased loved one where friends and family can leave a message, memory, or note of condolence. The idea of *e-burol* is a decade old, introduced in 2009 because of increased customer demand, as generations of Filipinos have continued to migrate for work to meet global demand and domestic economic needs.[8] The streaming service is available in forty chapels. In addition, according to one online reviewer, "Users may also chat with other relatives and visitors who are currently online while witnessing the wake. St. Peter has provided a 4-page guide, complete with photos in order [to] help clients access E-Burol."[9] That is, just like any chat board, mourners from afar can have conversations among themselves as they watch the proceedings. The funeral home provides a link and a password good for the length of the wake, which can last anywhere from two to ten days. From their computer, the e-mourner, so to speak, can be "there" to grieve remotely with the family.

George and I sat in the living room watching the screen. The funeral viewing room expanded into the living room spatially, with the camera in the Philippines and the laptop monitor in the United States. The camera seemed to be positioned where two walls met the ceiling, since the casket was at the bottom of the screen and at an angle. We heard no ambient sound, since there was no microphone provided. Too much bandwidth. The camera framed the scene, a frame that kept my friend to the side atop a wall from the perspective of the mourners in the room. Clearly, the screen on his laptop could not include him in it. Yet he was the person who had made the ritual event, both physical and virtual, possible through his cash remittance. The wake and funeral together would cost anywhere between 150,000PhP and 250,000PhP ($3,000 to $5,000). Because it was a one-way camera, as he watched the room, the mourners there could not see him. If he were physically in Manila, he would be accepting condolences, and his presence would be acknowledged and reflected with other family members. In that scenario of acknowledgment he too would be able to see himself being with others, but not in this feed. In the physical viewing room, he was the unseen, unheard, disembodied presence looking down at the body and the mourners. During the rest of week-long wake back at his university, he was physically either alone in his office or with people who might otherwise not know about his loss. In both places, the grieving part of himself was not given a public face.[10]

The digital feed enables a synchronization of time zones and spaces, but the visual framing also effects erasures or gaps in vision. While visualization of the ritual provides some comfort, the frame renders the viewer absent. The camera as a technological addition to the viewing room represents and makes present those who are unable to attend, particularly the one whose funds and labor constituted the gathering. Both the money and its source that made the event possible are felt in the viewing room. Neither can be fully acknowledged, on screen and off, but neither the individual nor the funds are the sole engines that constitute the ritual. I note the economic relationship but caution against giving the indisputably potent outside (call it capital, imperialism, global mediascapes, etc.) too much power in determining the script, blocking, action, stage directions, and meanings of this ritual. The technological affordance reveals tensions between "here" and "there" while also expanding possibilities between absence and presence, sociality and communality, and private and public grief. Other potencies are at play, and subjects are not mere vessels through which discourses and images flow to discipline behavior and perspectives.

Grieving is a relational act. The act of grieving, alone or with others, makes palpable the vulnerable sites that selves usually keep at bay to preserve our notions of individuality. Grief reminds us, as Judith Butler puts it, of "the ways in which we are, from the start and by virtue of being a bodily being, already given over, beyond ourselves, implicated in lives not our own."[11] A *burol* is the communal ritual of grieving and mourning to make evident the social network of the deceased, making manifest their personhood as an ecology of people and meanings. To gather in this moment of vulnerability is testament to the deceased having lived with and through others. To be sure, the social ecology is riven with all the conflicts, inequity, ambivalence, and violence that bring subjects and technological platforms together. *E-burol* indexes and enables types of presences and self-presentations that shape the social network of meanings around the deceased's life and the mourners' lives. The technology, power asymmetries, and capital flows all constitute the very environment by which dividuals—not separate individuals but bodily beings implicated in others—constitute communalities through various self-presentations.

The use of the technology generates *pakiramdam*, to be felt as a presence that subtly shifts the mood of the room. I would underscore how this feel and presence do not grow out of intention but is also in concert with what the people in the physical viewing room attribute to the medium. The meaning of the camera atop the wall ranged from a glamorous ghost or visiting spirit requiring a human medium to a low-tech supplement to text messages or a live broadcast to the United States. Over the week, this technologically mediated interaction with guests and family members coming from different parts of the country produced a host of reactions. My friend's mother "would even get dressed up when she knew [he] was coming on [camera]." Even though his presence was nonvisual, nonauditory, and nonhaptic, the mere knowledge of his eventual arrival occasioned transformation, dressing up. However, the idea of America—as the source of movies and luxury goods, as the preferred destination of many Filipino migrants over decades, not to mention its imperial history over the archipelago—was also in play. *That* America coming into the viewing room also occasioned her special preparations. Despite having no sensorial indicator, the son and "America" emitted auras of potency unseen from "out there." And "out there" was entwined psychically, intimately, and emotionally in this very private ritual so as to effect a different feel in the room.

For George's mother, being broadcast abroad even for an audience of one entailed a formality of staged performance, involving an appropriate outfit change. Philippine popular imagination would associate the live-feed medium with reality TV shows like *Pinoy Big Brother*, the local version of the North American and Australian reality-surveillance show. For sure, her "dressing up" was for the son who had been a major financial support for the family. The camera going "live" also changed the mother's perception of the room. So, some foreign place was not simply coming *into* the room; even more importantly for the mother and guests, the local images were being broadcast *out*. The mother's self-presentation in her view would have to be suitable for both person and place as potencies that reshaped the occasion. George's mother was right to dress up: One never knows who might be watching. The camera, acknowledged from time to time at the behest of the sister, transformed the ritual of receiving guests into a live broadcast of an intimate reality show for an imagined audience of one or a few. The formality or self-consciousness of being "on TV," albeit a computer screen in this case, gave the event a patina of glamour—

real because it was mediated through an imagined "TV" camera with an American audience watching.

Despite this power imbalance, only when the guests at St. Peter on-screen, acknowledged the audience could the social loop be completed. Because there was no sound, the sister had double duty as host and vocal (and bodily) conduit for the texts from George. Indeed, she was family host, director, and medium. The script in interacting with the show's guests was altered slightly by the addition of this electronic textual inter-action. When George would text his sister asking about this or that guest as they came in, "'Hi daw,' my sister would tell them. Then they look up at the camera and wave to me." Upon being recognized by the formless entity hosting from out there, the guest often felt compelled to give a cur-sory wave to acknowledge the foreign, digital presence represented by the camera at the top corner of the room. The attendees all became part of the staging of mourning itself. More crucially for the viewer abroad, the mourners in the frame acknowledged him. The hand wave or any acknowl-edgment of the viewer welcomed him into the communal fold. This en-folding, rendered impossible given the limits of the technology there and what social mores would dictate, could be realized only when the view-er's screen responds back. Rather than online real time, the *real* vital time, was the moment of the hand wave to an unseen presence, the act of *paki-ramdam*, wherein acknowledgment of mutual presence transpired. The hand wave as acknowledgment needed the technology but also signaled the failure and limitations of the technology. The texts, phones, cameras, hand waves, the glamour, bemusement, and even delighted chuckles and surprise—human and technological material—were all part of the com-plex ecology of this virtual presence in mourning. Rather than an exclu-sionary practice through surveillance, the camera feed enabled the family member abroad to see acts of communing and, more crucially, to be ac-knowledged by that communality.

Kapiling: Modulating Presence and Proximity

The week-long vigil in the Philippines as a twenty-four-hour activity involves family members taking eight-hour shifts for the duration, since the deceased's body must always be accompanied by loved ones until transport to its final physical and spiritual resting place.[12] An important aspect of *e-burol* is not just the opportunities to connect with family, as in US practice, but rather the times when there is no interaction between the two juxtaposed spaces. Everyday work happens in one place while ritual time happens on screen. Over the week, George was content to see the funereal world only occasionally: "I would leave the camera on as they went about greeting guests or arranging things. Over here, I was making dinner, doing laundry, eating, watching. If I were there physically, time would stop. This way my everyday still goes on." He can be "around" without engaging fully. This way he could manage entry into and out of the ritual time and into everyday time. All the while the family and loss would be physically evident as a computer screen on the office or kitchen table. By being present when nothing particular was happening in the physical viewing room or between him and the room, the virtual proximity, or *kapiling*, without the burden of family or social expectations, gave comfort and the space to manage personal grief alone while being with others. Being physically present would require stopping to observe ritual duties.

This practice in *kapiling* acknowledges the loss and its attendant rituals without engaging fully or being fully lost in it as a feeling. The practice has larger implications. Mourning is difficult. So are families. To be with but not engage fully in physical and emotional ways through this technology also means not having to engage with larger social structures, not just family but also the state, economic forces, and the law. For queer subjects, for migrants both documented and undocumented, for those in various economic and legal precarities, these larger structures can pose challenges. In one sense, to stop is to be undone not just by mourning but by the structural demands of mourning. The person might not be allowed to return to work or to the host country if they were to leave. Crossing the border might be the subject's undoing, given legal and economic limitations. For a queer subject, putting on a heteronormative face for family might also undo the world any migrant subject has been able to create elsewhere. Any action or feeling apart from the group or that departs from social expectations becomes impossible. To be undone by grief and mourning can be personal as well as structural.

Thus I read the desire to maintain the everyday distinct as stemming from the structures that the migrant has created to keep at bay the destructive demands that family, social normativity, the state, and the economy continue to inflict. By containing the ritual in one corner, the viewer manages what would otherwise be an overwhelming pull of family, social, legal, and economic disciplines. Here, surveillance as figured in the camera and monitor is not quite the same disciplining apparatus as that in the Foucauldian prison house. Rather than illuminating that which requires exclusion and discipline at the center, this particular camera is focused on the periphery of life itself and, in the global South, locations and subjects already rendered disposable and excluded.[13] In these peripheral visions, we can locate those timely frictions that allow spaces for other life-times to be lived.

For many migrants, the virtual might feel like a poor substitute. Physical presence is certainly preferred. However, all forms of presence do matter here, as in the scenarios described in this Coda. The sole demand in this ritual of laying a loved one to rest by family and friends is simply to show up. In this ritual, all types of presence—physical, virtual, ghostly, and imagined—are matters of consolation. Not doing so risks disturbing the smooth functioning of this social ecology, summarized in the oft-thought query: What would the neighbors say? In Filipino culture, *hiya* (shame) and *utang na loob* (debt of obligation) control sociality and communal rituals. Both concepts determine both the material and immaterial obligations to maintain group cohesion. The reading of absence and presence of and by various community and family members and the social functions and obligations each is presumed to have are continually up for discussion, as any family gathering would attest. Through the nonvisual, faceless presence, one can in fact "save face," as the next best thing—for everyone.

E-burol is a delivery system of presence and affect that provides the qualitative recompense to qualitative communal demands of shame, debt of obligation, and consolation. These demands all mark a lack in the social ecology that requires acts of recovery, but as qualitative and relational terms they also index the impossibility of recoverability itself. No amount of remittance of goods or funds in the economistic sense can make up for the shortfall, especially one precipitated by death. Butler reminds us that the only real grief worth its name is that which has no recompense or consolation. The decedent can never be replaced, after all. No amount of consolation can truly console. Nothing, not even physical presence, will ever be enough. While one might rightly understand long-distance grieving as an effect of capitalism's violence, what I read here alongside this fact is the possibility of varied intensities of mourning and relating differently to loss as well as to family and other communal structures. People might be engrouped differently, in more layered, loose, or tactical ways, not just in the conventional ways of being together.

Kapiling and *pakiramdam* as types of feelings that modulate being with others are not necessarily unique to Filipino culture, but the words encapsulate in everyday parlance the variety of ways to generate fellow-feeling, communality, and with-ness without subjects having to occupy time and space in alignment or at once, a condition of the labor diaspora. If virtual presence marks lack, then such a hierarchy of being with also instantiates multiple ways of being with. The imagined connection at the moment, rather than hearing about an event like a funeral after the fact, is considered superior to texting, which suffers a time lag, despite being in almost real time. The visual, though imagined only on one side, in turn has priority over text in terms of immediacy. To share the moment, that is, to share time together, seeks to erase the difference, the shortcoming, physical distance makes. More broadly, given the power asymmetries within diaspora, these modulations inform possibilities of engagement within differing systems that structure how life is lived. These ways of being with others are communicative, affective relationalities not easily quantified or even rationalized. More critically, they do not presume self-realized sovereign individuals with full agential volition or intent of engagement, for such is not the privilege of labor in the diaspora and other marginalized subjects.

As with the young men in the fan video which began this book, "to be beside oneself" is not only an emotional state but an index of intensity. Linguistically, the idiom implies that one is doubled or that one has been excised from one's own body. It is also a "state," a temporary way of being split from one's usual self-knowledge. Besideness here does not simply signify emotional excess but marks the production of proximities not just mediated but modulated and textured. Privileging knowledge produced in moments wherein senses are misaligned (when one is beside oneself) and when one is "unhinged" generates different ways of looking at relations between oneself and the world. Reaching out to one another, reaching out to friends via text, reaching out to the rest of the world via internet connectivity, reaching out in time to memory making and posterity as the present instantiates its own affective dispersal: The technological affordance disperses social norms toward a different mode of affective exchange. Remote grieving is an improvisational deployment of self, tools, and time. To gather duration and imagination signals vitality and affective exchange alongside but also beyond capitalist intention and national borders to achieve legibility to one another even in dis-articulation. Massumi suggests that capitalism is an open system of enfolding potentialities, so "capitalism is aspirationally all-taking. But that does not mean that everything is given to it."[14] By insisting upon capitalism as an open processual system that modulates potential and futurity, he leaves it possible to imagine interstitial and uncaptured activity even in creative activity embedded in capital relations.

In explicating Heidegger's view of worlding in the case for literature, Pheng Cheah notes that rather than an encounter with objects, worlding is relationality itself, the always-already collective.[15] World is continually being made and remade, and as such he underscores the "fundamental distinction between a spatio-geographical entity and the world as an ongoing work." In describing postcolonial openings, Cheah rehearses Fanon's argument about the temporality of decolonization as a refashioning of the precolonial past not to ossify it, as colonizers have done successfully, but to fashion for a nation a new future. Fanon indexes biological rhythms of struggle as consonant with cultural struggle: "He cannot conceive his life otherwise than as a kind of combat against exploitation; misery and hunger," Cheah quotes from *Wretched of the Earth*.[16] The body's struggle with the rhythms of capital, empire, racism, and other powers constitutes the making of culture in the locale. The struggle itself is a desire for an opening to a different future. Cheah uses literary genres for strategies to characterize postcolonial openings: epic and drama. Epic is the globalization approach that takes the view from above shaping the local; drama is the intercultural agon on the ground that offers the resistance.[17] He looks elsewhere to ask what mediations are available to local actors by which they imagine and act in the world, as "it is necessary to maintain the surprise and allow for multiple narrations."[18] While he privileges literature for its nonplacedness, I would hasten to add that the creative deployments of time explored in this book allow such glimpses into such openings because they offer not only other ways to feel time together but the surprises that allow multiple narrations.[19]

This book seeks to name and make legible possibilities for meaning making and lifeways generated alongside capital relations that might harness these activities as "socially necessary" but whose meanings and relations are not fully determined by them. These forms of communing reveal ways of experiencing time with another. In the bending, disruption, and frictions in time, these life-making activities through modes of exchange and accumulation without profit manifest in these affective communal worlds, momentary but palpable gatherings of the imagination.

Acknowledgments

"Filipino time!" or "Pinoy time!" is exclaimed in exasperation by Filipinos when friends show up or events begin hours later than arranged. Everyone expects an interminable wait, caused by traffic, outfit changes, or an eyebrow not quite drawn right. Some lie about meeting times to repeat offenders, who know they are being lied to anyway, causing even more delays. Filipino time is never one's fault. It is simply a way of living, an erratic cadence embedded and embodied in the everyday.

As with Filipino time, expressions of gratitude come always a tad too late. They tarry after the felt sentiment itself. Communities of generous and creative thinkers, doers, producers, and fellow travelers paved paths and made imaginable the ways to complete this book. All the book's shortcomings are mine.

My gratitude and respect to the kind Filipino families and individuals who took me in and opened their hearts, homes, and magic mics in Tel Aviv. *Maraming salamat* to the staff at the Philippine consulate in Tel Aviv. Thank you to Chiqui and the original Paper Dolls in London and Brighton for sharing their stories with me and the rest of the world. Hats off to Maribel Legarda, Lisa Magtoto, the PETA Library and Archives, and the collective that is PETA for their unmatched vision, generosity, and commitment. My thanks to Leeroy New and his bold activism and artwork, which graces the cover of this book, from his series Aliens of Manila. The image here is evocative of a different Venus, one rising in turbulent waters. Across many bodies of water, my debt of gratitude to cousins spread across Manila, Cebu, Toronto, Sydney, Dubai, and California, who are themselves teachers, caregivers, call center workers, and health care workers, for thinking, talking, and laughing with me. *Maraming salamat* to Che-Che and all the call center folks in Cebu and Manila who were so willing to share themselves during their early morning dinner times and on their days off. I am responsible to you all.

My *utang na loob* to interlocutors over many years on- and offline beside me or at the side of my computer screen guiding me: Martin Manalansan for always being a generative, scholarly force; Lucy San Pablo Burns and Christine Bacareza Balance for reading drafts at different turns and offering their keen insights; Bill Johnson-Gonzalez, Anita Mannur, and Donette Francis for their always provocative exchange of ideas; Robert Diaz and Denise Cruz for bringing together in Canada and the United States so much fierce beauty of thought and people in panels with Genevieve Clutario, Thuy Lin Tu, Ferdie Lopez, and Gary Devilles; Khoi Luu for keeping me up to date on Miss Universe year in, year out; and Christine, Zack, Lucy, Robert, and Robyn Rodriguez, who brought many homes together as fellow travelers in the traffic of ideas, the traffic in Manila, and in traversing across islands, hills, and mountains. I invoke the memory and power of Amado Khaya Canham-Rodriguez, who created timeless worlds we can only want in those islands, hills, and mountains.

I thank Yao-Fen You, Jeff Rebudal, R. Zamora Linmark, Mark Berkowitz, Peter Mayshle, Mike Santos, Christine Duque, and Laylah Ali for providing sustenance, drink, joy, and a sense of home. Many thanks to the New York Asian American Studies group, James Kim, Elda Tsou, Thuy Lin Tu, and Jeffrey Santa Ana, for reading through concepts in their rough preliminary stages; Sarita See for her perspicacity and encouragement from idea to completion; Henry Abelove for decades of humor, dinners, and delight; Cathy Schlund-Vials for her unwavering support and intellectual generosity; and Richard Morrison for his vision and patience these many years.

My gratitude to my colleagues in the American Studies Department at Rutgers for imagining life and work differently, particularly to Ben Sifuentes-Jáuregui and Lou Masur. Thank you to Ji Lee and Rick Lee for being unfailing comrades. My appreciation to the tireless research assistants who were generous with their time and intellect: Alison Boldero, Camille Ungco, Rachel Landingin, and Edward Nadurata. I am thankful for the support of the Rutgers Office of Research, the Institute for Research on Women, and the Center for Cultural Analysis for support in developing early stages of the research. I am indebted to the sustained dialogue around archipelagoes with Yolanda Martínez-San Miguel and Michelle Stephens. Thank you to all who invited me to share parts of the work and provided invaluable feedback that have shaped my thoughts: Philippine

Women's University; the J. Elizalde Navarro Workshop in Theory and Criticism, University of Santo Tomas, Philippines; Crystal Parikh at the NYU Asian/Pacific/American Institute; Laurel Mei-Singh and Nijah Cunningham at Princeton University; Stan Thangaraj and Angie Reyes at CUNY's Future of Asian American Studies conference; Kandice Chuh at the CUNY Graduate Center; David Eng for his wonderful queries; Victor Bascara, who provocatively asked years ago if I thought Filipinos inhabited another temporality, setting me off on this path; and the wonderful fellows and leaders of the Charles Warren Center seminar, who inspired the final lap that opened to the next set of adventures.

I am indebted to the memory and work of my parents, Lorenzo and Felicidad Punzalan Isaac, but also look forward to the timeless worlds to be revealed and created by their grandchildren: Allyson, Tina, Jillian, Nicole, Liane, and Justin.

Notes

Introduction: Accumulating Time

1. Rey Chow, *Entanglements, or Transmedial Thinking about Capture* (Durham, NC: Duke University Press, 2012), 165.

2. In the end, the twenty-two-year-old brown beauty took fourth runner-up after her disastrous answer in the final round of questions. Diane Sawyer, a former beauty queen contestant herself, would later comment: "No answer, no crown." The favored-to-win beauty queen's final answer cost her the crown, and the phrase "major, major" became part of Philippine popular cultural idiom.

3. Ben O. De Vera, "Cash Sent by OFWs Hit Record-High $2.55B in December—BSP," *Inquirer.net*, February 17, 2017.

4. Ben O. De Vera, "OFW Remittances up 5.5% to $2.3B in May," *Inquirer.net*, July 18, 2017.

5. This does not account for those who emigrate or overstay their authorized entry visas.

6. The young men's exuberance as pure spectators was infectious, as the word "viral" in "viral video" suggests. Not only had there been over two million hits; there had been spoofs (by white Americans, by Filipino Americans, by presumably straight-acting men) and a KFC commercial in the Philippines for popcorn chicken. The video's compelling nature both makes one want to watch it over and over again and inspires others to relive, to reembody, the ecstasy in some way. None of these copies gets at the same level and quality of excitement as the original. In our desire to get at the subtle emergence of unthinking reactions, even those grossly private, the original still retains its aura.

7. I recognize that "going viral" partakes in noneconomic exchanges, but the views, likes, comments, reposts, and other circulations on text platforms are also quantified and monetized.

8. Michel Foucault, "Of Other Spaces: Utopias and Heterotopias," trans. Jay Miskowiec, *Diacritics* 16, no. 1, (Spring 1986): 22–27.

9. Chow, *Entanglements*, 167.

10. Walter Benjamin, "The Work of Art in the Age of Mechanical Reproduction," in *Illuminations*, trans. Harry Zohn (New York: Schocken, 1969).

11. See Elizabeth Freeman, *Beside You in Time: Sense-Methods and Queer Sociabilities in Nineteenth-Century America* (Durham, NC: Duke University Press, 2019). In Freeman's reframing, "chronics" are those who possess other sensibilities around time: "People whose queerness inheres in their relation to time, not as forward- or backward-moving but as ebbing and flowing in varying degrees of intensity and insistence, compression and dilation, irreducible to the habits that consolidate identity" (146).

12. José Esteban Muñoz, *Cruising Utopia: The Then and There of Queer Futurity* (New York: New York University Press, 2009), 27.

13. Muñoz, *Cruising Utopia*, 185. Muñoz meditates upon the word and experience of ecstasy: "*Ekstasis*, in the ancient Greek (*exstare* in the Latin), means 'to stand' or 'to be out outside of oneself,' *ex* meaning 'out' and *stasis* meaning 'stand.' . . . Knowing ecstasy is having a sense of timeliness's motion, comprehending a temporal unity, which includes the past (having-been), the future (not-yet), and the present (the making-present)" (186).

14. Rachel Aviv, "The Cost of Caring: The Lives of the Immigrant Women Who Tend to the Needs of Others," *New Yorker*, April 4, 2016. I note that a year before, the *Atlantic* published an article posthumously by Alex Tizon in its June 2017 issue sensationalistically entitled, "My Family's Slave." Tizon passed away in March that year. The Tizon article seems to rehearse for me American innocence in a family that has lived off the unpaid labor of an aging servant named Eudocia Tomas Pulido, affectionately called "Lola," or "grandmother." While the article tells of tragic labor exploitation, it fails to distinguish among types of unfreedoms, eliding the practice of chattel slavery and enslaved Africans with feudal exploitation. Feudal relations in the Philippines worked seamlessly with neocolonialism, wage-work subsistence, and citizenship and border precarities that brought the family and Lola to the United States. US immigration and labor laws further exacerbated and obscured Lola's exploitative relationship with the family. The seemingly unedited article by Tizon points to how American dreams are historically and currently built on many forms of racialized and gendered labor exploitation. I would add, however, that the global North has managed to outsource forms of enslavement outside its borders, rendering these relations out of sight, so that many of us in the United States can enjoy our consumer and other "freedoms" without the burden of direct association with and responsibility for them.

15. Aviv, "The Cost of Caring."

16. Theodore S. Gonzalves, *The Day the Dancers Stayed: Performing in the Filipino/American Diaspora* (Philadelphia: Temple University Press, 2010), 22. Gonzalves points to social science work by Jonathan Okamura, Rhacel Parreñas, Yen Le Espiritu, Rick Bonus, Emily Ignacio, and Martin Manalansan, among others. In literary and cultural studies, Jeffrey Santa Ana offers an in-depth exploration of Asian American racialization in late capitalism in *Racial Feelings: Asian America in a Capitalist Culture of Emotion* (Philadelphia: Temple University Press, 2015).

17. Michael Hardt, "Affective Labor," *boundary 2* 26, no. 2 (Summer 1999): 93.

18. Robyn Magalit Rodriguez, *Migrants for Export: How the Philippine State Brokers Labor to the World* (Minneapolis: University of Minnesota Press, 2010), xiii.

19. See Sara Ahmed, "Orientations: Toward a Queer Phenomenology," *GLQ: Journal of Lesbian and Gay Studies* 12, no. 4 (2006): 543–74. Elaborating on the "orientation" that a body inhabits, Ahmed provides a directional dimension to discursive citation: "We could recall here that Judith Butler, following Louis Althusser, makes 'turning' crucial to subject formation. One becomes a subject through 'turning around' when hailed by the police. For Butler, this 'turning' takes the form of hearing oneself as the subject of address: It is a turning that is not really about physicality of movement (1997c:33). But we can make the question of direction crucial to the emergence of subjectivity and the 'force' of the given name. In other words, we could reflect on the difference it makes which way subjects turn." Ahmed's orientation refers to Butler's citationality in reference to gender and sexuality to describe the texture of the field the body feels and acts upon within discursive hailing.

20. Eve Sedgwick, "Queer Performativity: Henry James's Art of the Novel," *GLQ: Journal of Lesbian and Gay Studies* 1, no. 1 (1993): 1–16.

21. Eve Kosofsky Sedgwick, *Touching Feeling: Affect, Pedagogy, Performance* (Durham, NC: Duke University Press, 2003), 8.

22. Sedgwick, *Touching Feeling*, 8.

23. "Services of proximity," Hardt observes in affective work, "are the creation and manipulation of affect." Hardt, "Affective Labor," 293.

24. Vital energies, according to Kalindi Vora, are "the substance of activity that produce life (though often deemed reproductive)—from areas of life depletion to areas of life enrichment." Kalindi Vora, *Life Support: Biocapital and the New History of Outsourced Labor* (Minneapolis: University of Minnesota Press, 2015), 3. Thus biocapital resources could be alienated and transferred to the global North from the global South. This continuation of colonial relations, Vora argues, depletes the lives of service providers by mobilizing parts of their bodies to enrich the lives of the capital-rich consumer. Vora notes in her history of biocapital extraction from surrogacy to call centers that living labor, after Marx, "doesn't rely on quantifying expenditure (labor-time) but rather on this subjective marking of what is exhausted." While an accurate characterization in terms of the worker, this formulation does not quite explore the qualitative life- and meaning-making capacity of the subject herself despite mandatory exhaustion by employer demands. Socially necessary labor time requires the continual production of social worlds that must be sustained as part of that expenditure.

25. Brian Massumi, *99 Theses on the Revaluation of Value: A Postcapitalist Manifesto* (Minneapolis: University of Minnesota Press, 2018). Massumi suggests that "the more adequate perspective is to treat the individual as a dividual: a composition of proto-subjective tendencies in tension and concertation" (61).

26. Sara Ahmed, *Queer Phenomenology: Orientations, Objects, Others* (Durham, NC: Duke University Press, 2006).

27. In *The Intimacies of Four Continents*, Lowe looks at nineteenth-century phenomena through which we understand lost possibilities that merchant colonialism had cobbled together in its control of trade, objects, and peoples. Lowe defines intimacy on several scales—proximity, political coalition, privacy, and sexuality—as generative of communal narratives as alternative spaces to settler nation-state formations. What Lowe recovers in exploring these simultaneous intimacies found in the early nineteenth century is a memory of a future, a stored

potential, that Massumi suggests is called upon later, as so-called usable pasts. Lisa Lowe, *The Intimacies of Four Continents* (Durham, NC: Duke University Press, 2015).

28. Arlie Hochschild, *The Managed Heart: Commercialization of Human Feeling* (Berkeley: University of California Press, 1983), 70.

29. Sarita Echavez See, *The Filipino Primitive: Accumulation and Resistance in the American Museum* (New York: New York University Press, 2017). What See uncovers is the process of making "primitives" in settler-colonial logic first by evacuating land and then by evacuating knowledge about land and social relations. The making of the primitive is the way settler capitalism can not only exile the colonized from land but also from history. Rather than locating this moment of expulsion in primeval history, this dispossession of land and knowledge is a continual process, as Rosa Luxembourg points out. People, land, and time must be produced and prepared for capture.

30. Massimiliano Tomba, *Marx's Temporalities* (Leiden: Brill, 2012), 161.

31. In response to leftist activist goals to disalienate labor, in her example, encouraging workers to bring their uniqueness into the workplace is about flexibility to improve participation but also leads workers to internalize the organizational discipline, leading to "work intensification": "In a kind of bad dialectic, quality becomes quantity as the call for better work is translated into a requirement for more work." Flexibility and uniqueness become part of the job description. Making work more "fulfilling" or not alienated operates toward perfecting the systems of productivity and production: "The affirmation of unalienated labor is not an adequate strategy by which to contest contemporary modes of capitalist control; it is too readily co-opted in a context in which the metaphysics of labor and the moralization of work carries so much cultural authority in so many realms." Kathi Weeks, *The Problem with Work: Feminism, Marxism, Antiwork Politics, and Postwork Imaginaries* (Durham, NC: Duke University Press, 2011), 107.

32. Attending to the tensions between alienated and alien labor, Day rethinks Marx's labor theory of value to query the conditions of what is "socially necessary" in labor-time under the settler-colonial mode of production. She argues that the initial abstraction of labor itself is the primary violence that makes dispossession possible. She points more urgently to the control of the social and the everyday, in which racial and gendered difference is rendered a social necessity for the dispossession and assignment of value. "Nothing prevents racial engendered labor from being a social necessity that determines average labor time," asserts Day. That is, while concurring with Lisa Lowe and David Roediger that capital continually creates surplus value through difference in race and gender hierarchies, the abstraction of labor into money is the preliminary violence necessary that erroneously separates concrete and abstract labor, giving rise to romantic anticapitalism. In Day's Canadian context, this intentional error is part of white settler logic to racialize financial capital: abstract labor assigned to Asian aliens, concrete labor to white settlers. The initial abstraction to make differential labor equivalent to money wages makes possible the circulation of workers' bodies for capital deployment. Iyko Day, *Alien Capital: Asian Racialization and the Logic of Settler Colonial Capitalism* (Durham, NC: Duke University Press, 2016).

33. Kalindi Vora has described how "the dual character of reproductive work within capitalism occurs because it represents itself and its subject bearer as

nonvalue, yet it simultaneously functions to siphon the value it produces into capital through the productive worker." Vora, *Life Support*, 54.

34. Neferti Tadiar, "Life-Times of Becoming Human," *Occasion: Interdisciplinary Studies in the Humanities* 3 (March 1, 2012).

35. Neferti Tadiar, "Decolonization, 'Race,' and Remaindered Life under Empire," in *Critical Ethnic Studies: A Reader*, ed. Nada Elia et al. (Durham, NC: Duke University Press, 2016), 408. Tadiar's work on Filipino culture and imagination founds many of my claims in this book. I heed the call by Tadiar to glean portions of "remaindered life," in an essay of the same name, that indexes "life-sustaining forms and practices of personhood and sociality" rendered unintelligible under imperial reproductions and economistic frames.

36. Franco "Bifo" Berardi, *The Soul at Work: From Alienation to Autonomy* (Cambridge, MA: MIT Press, 2009), 21.

37. Michael Hardt and Antonio Negri, *Empire* (Cambridge, MA: Harvard University Press, 2001), 301.

38. Hardt and Negri, *Empire*, 301.

39. Foucault, "Of Other Spaces," 26.

40. Foucault, "Of Other Spaces," 26.

41. Neferti Tadiar, "Life-Times in Fate Playing," *South Atlantic Quarterly* 111, no. 4 (Fall 2012): 796.

42. Grace Kyungwon Hong, "Speculative Surplus: Asian American Racialization and the Neoliberal Shift," *Social Text* 36, no. 2 (June 1, 2018): 111. This is apparent in the discourses of our universities that compel us to make explicit the use and exchange value of our humanities work and to articulate our time in the classroom as preparing students to be market ready and competitive in the global workplace. I read Hong's use of proliferation as that which is articulable only because it is directly translatable into capital's vernacular of supply and demand. Student time spent at university now is to be traded for a "better," read profitable, future.

43. Hardt, "Affective Labor," 96.

44. See Dipesh Chakrabarty, *Provincializing Europe: Postcolonial Thought and Historical Difference* (Princeton, NJ: Princeton University Press, 2000).

45. Gayatri Gopinath, *Unruly Visions* (Durham, NC: Duke University Press, 2018), 7.

46. Ana Romina Guevarra, *Marketing Dreams, Manufacturing Heroes: The Transnational Labor Brokering of Filipino Workers* (New Brunswick, NJ: Rutgers University Press, 2009); Rodriguez, *Migrants for Export*; Catherine Ceniza Choy, *Empire of Care: Nursing and Migration in Filipino American History* (Durham, NC: Duke University Press, 2003).

47. Stefano Harney and Fred Moten, *The Undercommons: Fugitive Planning and Black Study* (Wivenhoe: Minor Compositions, 2013), 98.

48. Harney and Moten, *The Undercommons*.

1 / "I've Never Been to Me": Redirecting Arrivals and Returns

1. In 2017, 2,800 foreign teachers entered the United States under J-1 visas to fill the shortages. J-1 visas are cultural exchange visas used in the hotel and education industries and are more insecure than H1-B work visas. As Robyn Rodriguez has observed, these degrees of legality blur the lines between legal and illegal, secure and precarious (comments made on PALAD panel, May 23, 2020). The recruitment

continues amid the ever-continuing devaluation of the profession, as the wave of teacher walkouts in 2018 attests to. Dana Goldstein, "Teacher Pay Is So Low in Some US School Districts That They're Recruiting Overseas," *New York Times*, May 3, 2018.

2. See Lora Bartlett, *Migrant Teachers: How American Schools Import Labor* (Cambridge, MA: Harvard University Press, 2014).

3. *The Learning*, dir. Ramona Diaz, CineDiaz Inc., 2011.

4. I use Bill Nichols's classifications here. Bill Nichols, *Introduction to Documentary*, 2nd ed. (Bloomington: Indiana University Press, 2010).

5. Ramona Diaz, interview by author, June 3, 2017.

6. Bienvenido Lumbera, "'Dating': Panimulang Muni sa Estetika ng Panitikang Filipino," *Lagda 1* (1999): 34. I am grateful to Martin Manalansan for pointing me to this article.

7. Lumbera, "Dating," 33–42. My translation.

8. David Jonathan Bayot, "Bienvenido L. Lumbera on Revaluation: The National Stages of Philippine Literature and Its History," *IDEYA: Journal of Humanities* 8, no. 1 (2006): 106.

9. *Dating* is used in various ways in the vernacular to describe the negative and positive effect or impact of a person or object or even the potential to have an effect. *Dating*, noun, should not be confused with *dáting*, emphasis on the first syllable, an adjective that means past or former.

10. Benedict Anderson, *Language and Power: Exploring Political Cultures in Indonesia* (Ithaca, NY: Cornell University Press, 1990), 28.

11. Kandice Chuh, *The Difference Aesthetics Makes: On the Humanities "After Man"* (Durham, NC: Duke University Pres, 2019), 22. Chuh's work returns aesthetics to its minor keys by looking at the contradictions and tensions within what has been calcified and rarefied in terms of institutionalized criteria of judgment.

12. Bayot, "Bienvenido L. Lumbera on Revaluation."

13. Fenella Cannell, *Power and Intimacy in the Christian Philippines* (Cambridge: Cambridge University Press, 1999).

14. Martin Manalansan IV, *Global Divas: Filipino Gay Men in the Diaspora* (Durham, NC: Duke University Press, 2003), 186. "*Bakla*," as Manalansan signals in the Tagalog word for gay and gender-queer bodies and sensibilities, "invokes particular kinds of scripts that point to notions of self, embedded in social relations . . . *bakla* is not an identity that is assumed by particular men but more accurately a slippery condition, a performative event or series of events of self-formation."

15. Neferti Tadiar, "Life-Times of Disposability within Global Neoliberalism," *Social Text* 31, no. 2 (Summer 2013): 19–48. Tadiar has described how flexible labor is forced to perform free social reproductive labor at home, while being paid for social reproductive labor in the global North, thus producing capital for the Philippine national economy even as she serves the US service economy.

16. Sarita Echavez See, *The Filipino Primitive: Accumulation and Resistance in the American Museum* (New York: New York University Press, 2017), 119.

17. Charlene's ballad did not become a hit until its rerelease five years later in 1982. The song's overwrought emotionalism with its talking interlude made possible a popular resurgence in 1994, when it was used to open the Australian film hit *Adventures of Priscilla Queen of the Desert* (1994), about drag queens venturing out to perform in the Australian bush.

18. Ramona Diaz, interview by author, June 3, 2017.

19. Ramona Diaz, interview by author, June 3, 2017.

20. Some Filipino/American novels dealing with returns include Gina Apostol, *Insurrecto: A Novel* (New York: Soho, 2018); Peter Bacho, *Cebu* (Seattle: University of Washington Press, 1991); Jessica Hagedorn, *Dogeaters* (New York: Penguin, 1991); R. Zamora Linmark, *Leche* (Minneapolis: Coffee House, 2011); Han Ong, *The Disinherited* (New York: Farrar, Straus and Giroux, 2004); Randy Ribay, *Patron Saints of Nothing* (New York: Kokila, 2019); Michelle Cruz Skinner, *Balikbayan: A Filipino Homecoming* (Honolulu: Bess, 2008); Miguel Syjuco, *Ilustrado* (New York: Picado, 2010); Tif Marcelo, *Once upon a Sunset* (New York: Gallery, 2020). Recent scholarly work complicating returns include Eric Pido, *Migrant Returns: Manila, Development, and Transnational Connectivity* (Durham, NC: Duke University Press, 2017); Robert Diaz, "Failed Returns: The Queer Balikbayan in R. Zamora Linmark's *Leche* and Gil Portes's *Miguel Michelle*," in *Global Asian American Popular Cultures*, ed. Shilpa Davé, Leilani Nishime, and Tasha Oren (New York: NYU Press, 2016), 335–50; Martin Manalansan, "Wayward Erotics: Mediating Queer Diasporic Return," in *Media, Erotics, and Transnational Asia*, ed. Purnima Mankekar and Louisa Schein (Durham, NC: Duke University Press, 2012).

21. See Jose Antonio Vargas, *Dear America* (2018) and *Documented* (2014). The theme may not always be solely about the fantasy of return but also include the precarities of contemporary contract labor, including termination, debt peonage, expirations of visas, unauthorized entries, among others. Thanks to Lucy Burns for this insight regarding return narratives.

22. Benito Vergara, *Pinoy Capital: The Filipino Nation in Daly City* (Philadelphia: Temple University Press, 2009), 4.

23. See Gayatri Gopinath, *Impossible Desires: Queer Diasporas and South Asian Public Cultures* (Durham, NC: Duke University Press, 2005); and her recent work in *Unruly Visions* (Durham, NC: Duke University Press, 2018). I heed the call by Gopinath's definition of queer diaspora as remapping these cartographies as well as a way to reorient "the traditionally backward glance of conventional articulations of diaspora, often predicated on a desire for a return to lost origins" in *Unruly Visions*, 6.

24. Saloni Mathur, *The Migrant's Time: Rethinking Art History and Diaspora* (Williamstown, MA: Sterling and Francine Clark Art Institute, 2011), ix.

25. Ranajit Guha, "The Migrant's Time," *Postcolonial Studies: Culture, Politics, Economy* 1, no. 2 (1998): 156.

26. Guha, "The Migrant's Time," 156.

27. "People use songs and karaoke to define themselves and influence others." Rob Drew, *Karaoke Nights: An Ethnographic Rhapsody* (Walnut Creek, CA: Altamira, 2001); qtd. in Christine Bacareza Balance, *Tropical Renditions: Making Musical Scenes in Filipino America* (Durham, NC: Duke University Press, 2016), 71.

28. For more on 1970s ballads and Filipino trans-Pacific uses in performance, see Karen Tongson, *Why Karen Carpenter Matters* (Austin: University of Texas Press, 2019).

29. Lucy Mae San Pablo Burns, *Puro Arte: Filipinos on the Stages of Empire* (New York: New York University Press, 2013).

30. Patrick Flores, "Palabas," *Ctrl +P Journal of Contemporary Art*, March 2008, 9.

31. Balance, *Tropical Renditions*, 72.

32. Lumbera, "Dating." My italics.

33. Neferti X. Tadiar, *Fantasy-Production: Sexual Economies and Other Philippine Consequences for the New World Order* (Manila: Ateneo de Manila University Press, 2004).

34. "What the worker consumes over and above that minimum for his own pleasure is seen as unproductive consumption." Karl Marx, *Capital*, vol. 1, trans. Ben Fowkes (London: Penguin, 1976), 718.

2 / "Holding Out for Something Better": Timing and Other In-Between Times

1. Michelle Cruz Skinner, *In the Company of Strangers* (Honolulu: Bamboo Ridge), 119.

2. Paolo Virno, "The Ambivalence of Disenchantment," in *Radical Thought in Italy: A Potential Politics*, ed. Paolo Virno and Michael Hardt (Minneapolis: University of Minnesota Press, 1964), 16–17. I thank James Kim for directing me to this essay and his insights on ambivalence.

3. Many late-twentieth- and twenty-first-century Filipino diasporic literary works are informed by the great numbers of Filipinas exported for labor by the Philippine state. Alden Marte-Wood, "Philippine Reproductive Fiction and Crises of Social Reproduction," *Post 45* 1 (2019). Marte-Wood terms as "reproductive fictions" works that focus on the OFW service laborers as protagonists and minor characters.

4. Mia Alvar's short story "Miracle Worker" appears in her collection *In the Country: Stories* (New York: Knopf, 2015), about overseas Filipino workers (OFWs) and emigrants and set in Bahrain, the United States, and the Philippines. Skinner's "In the Company of Strangers" is a short story triptych in a collection of the same name. Go's flash fiction appears in the online magazine *American Short Fiction*.

5. Mary Louise Pratt, "The Short Story: The Long and the Short of It," *Poetics* 10 (1981): 175–94.

6. Paul Tillich, *The Eternal Now* (New York: Charles Scribner's Sons, 1963); qtd. in Roger Thompson, "Ralph Waldo Emerson and the American *Kairos*," in *Rhetoric and Kairos: Essays in History, Theory, and Praxis*, ed. Phillip Sipiora and James S. Baumlin (Albany: State University of New York Press), 188.

7. Amélie Frost Benedikt, "On Doing the Right Thing at the Right Time," in *Rhetoric and Kairos: Essays in History, Theory, and Praxis*, ed. Phillip Sipiora and James S. Baumlin (Albany: State University of New York Press), 226.

8. Virno, "The Ambivalence of Disenchantment," 21.

9. Grace Kyungwon Hong, "Speculative Surplus: Asian American Racialization and the Neoliberal Shift," *Social Text* 36, no. 2 (June 2018): 109.

10. David Harvey, *The Limits to Capital* (London: Verso, 1982), 266; qtd. in Hong, "Speculative Surplus."

11. Sarita Echavez See, "Lessons from the Illiterate: Carlos Bulosan and the Staged Wages of Romance," in *The Filipino Primitive* (New York: New York University Press, 2017).

12. Pierre Bourdieu, *The Logic of Practice*, trans. Richard Nice (Cambridge: Polity, 1990).

13. Gayatri Gopinath, *Unruly Visions: The Aesthetic Practice of Queer Diaspora* (Durham, NC: Duke University Press, 2018), 17.

14. Kathleen Stewart, *Ordinary Affects* (Durham, NC: Duke University Press, 2007), 129.

15. Latin *appositus*, past participle of *app-*, *adpōnĕre*, < *ad* to + *-pōnĕre* to place, put (*OED*). For example, an appositional phrase, a descriptive note such as this one, might serve as an emphatic or elucidation in the main clause.

16. Stefano Harney and Fred Moten, *The Undercommons: Fugitive Planning and Black Study* (Wivenhoe: Minor Compositions, 2013), 96.

17. Alvar, *In the Country*, 62.

18. The celebrated figure most associated with the term "Miracle Worker" is Annie Sullivan, the teacher of humble origins who led her student, the very privileged Helen Keller, from the darkness of being deaf and blind to graduate from Radcliffe.

19. Lisa Lowe, *The Intimacies of Four Continents* (Durham, NC: Duke University Press, 2015).

20. Race management, Roediger reminds us, precedes and founds industrial management. David Roediger, *The Production of Difference: Race and the Management of Labor in US History* (Oxford: Oxford University Press, 2012).

21. Marte-Wood describes how these minor characters analogize and enact the chain of care: "Functioning as mere recipients of a minor character's transnational reproductive care, Minnie's sisters and nieces (their gender seems an intentional detail) are the unrepresented end of a reproductive labor chain." Marte-Wood, "Philippine Reproductive Fiction."

22. Nathan Go, "Blind Oracle of Mactan," *American Short Fiction*, April 2, 2018, https://americanshortfiction.org/blind-oracle-mactan/.

23. See, *The Filipino Primitive*, 95.

3 / "I Understand Where You're Coming From": Temporal Migration and Offshore Chronographies

1. Karen Lerma, "Rise of Machines: Philippines Outsourcing Industry Braces for AI," *Reuters*, November 8, 2017.

2. Shane, interview by author, Manila, May 2012.

3. See Jan Padios, *A Nation on the Line: Call Centers as Postcolonial Predicaments in the Philippines* (Durham, NC: Duke University Press, 2018), an excellent ethnography that details the complex of immaterial labor extracted from call center agents in the Philippines as emergent global subjects. Purnima Mankekar's *Unsettling India* (Chapel Hill, NC: Duke University Press, 2015) touches on similar keywords—affect, temporality, and transnationality—with a focus on New Delhi and the Indian diaspora in the Bay Area, to examine call centers in India and the circulation and reception of films in the diaspora.

4. Espie Angelica A. De Leon, "IBPAP Eyes 1.8-M Jobs in IT-BPM Industry by 2022," *Newsbytes.PH*, April 22, 2018, http://newsbytes.ph/2018/04/22/ibpap-eyes-1-8-m-jobs-in-it-bpm-industry-by-2022.

5. Shalini Puri, "Finding the Field: Notes on Caribbean Cultural Criticism, Area Studies, and the Forms of Engagement," *Small Axe* 41, no. 2 (July 2013): 68–69.

6. Mankekar, *Unsettling India*.

7. Kalindi Vora, *Life Support: Biocapital and the New History of Outsourced Labor* (Minneapolis: University of Minnesota Press, 2015).

8. Alinaya Fabros, *Outsourceable Selves: An Ethnography of Call Center Work in a Global Economy of Signs and Selves* (Quezon City, Philippines: Ateneo de Manila University Press, 2016).

9. Padios, *A Nation on the Line*.

10. See Neferti Tadiar, *Fantasy-Production: Sexual Economies and Other Philippine Consequences for the New World Order* (Manila: Ateneo de Manila University Press, 2004).

11. Tess, interview by author, Manila, May 2012.

12. The model is Solen Heusaff, the daughter of a Filipina mother and French father, raised in the Philippines. She appeared in the reality show *Pinoy Big Brother* a few years before this photograph was taken.

13. Vora, *Life Support*, 51.

14. Brian Russell Roberts and Michelle Stephens, "Archipelagic American Studies and the Caribbean," *Journal of Transnational American Studies* 5, no. 1 (2013): 14.

15. Muhammad Munawwar, *Ocean States: Archipelagic Regimes in the Law of the Sea* (Dordrecht: Martinus Nijhoff, 1995), 62.

16. I thank Sarita See for this insight.

17. Pio Granada, "Last Minute Summer: Four Fantastic Quick Weekend Getaways," *After Call* 5, no. 2 (Midsummer 2012): 16.

18. "Work Abroad. Live Here," Facebook, https://www.facebook.com/WorkAbroad LiveHere.

19. Tess, interview by author, May 2012.

20. N. V. M. Gonzalez and Oscar V. Campomanes, "Filipino American Literature," in *An Interethnic Companion to Asian American Literature*, ed. King-Kok Cheung (Cambridge: Cambridge University Press, 1997), 100–1.

21. Jamaica Kincaid, *A Small Place* (New York: Farrar, Straus, Giroux, 1988), 18–19.

22. Raka Shome, "Thinking through the Diaspora: Call Centers, India, and a New Politics of Hybridity," *International Journal of Cultural Studies* 9, no. 1 (March 2006): 114.

23. "Carla" (call center agent), interview by author, Manila, June 2012.

24. Padios, *A Nation on the Line*, 5.

25. Vikas Bajaj, "A New Capital of Call Centers," *New York Times*, November 25, 2011.

26. Bajaj, "A New Capital of Call Centers."

27. Padios, *A Nation on the Line*, 11.

28. Tess, interview by author, Manila, May 2012.

29. Tess, interview by author, Manila, May 2012.

30. Rina, interview by author, Manila, June 2012.

31. Rina, interview by author, Manila, June 2012.

32. Boy, interview by author, Manila, June 2012.

33. Boy, interview by author, Manila, June 2012.

34. Boy, interview by author, Manila, June 2012.

35. Mankekar, *Unsettling India*, 189.

36. Shane, interview by author, Manila, June 2012.

37. Gina, interview by author, Manila, June 2012.

38. "BPOs to feel artificial intelligence 'reality' in next 3 to 5 years: Pernia," *ABS-CBN News*, January 24, 2018.

39. Shane, interview by author, Manila, July 2012.

40. Gina and Jane, interview by author, Manila, May 2012.

41. Shane, interview by author, Manila, June 2012.

42. Pio Granada, "BPOs: The Rise of the New Middle Class," 10–11.

43. Dan, Ben, and Carlo, interview by author, Cebu, July 2012.

44. Reena Patel, *Working the Night Shift: Women in India's Call Center Industry* (Stanford, CA: Stanford University Press, 2010), 145.

45. Jan Maghinay Padios, "Listening between the Lines: Culture, Difference, and Immaterial Labor in the Philippine Call Center Industry," PhD diss., New York University, 2012. See also "Queer Confessions: Transgression, Affect, and National Crisis in the Philippines' Call Center Industry," Center for Art + Thought, http://centerforartandthought.org.

46. Vicente Rafael, *The Promise of the Foreign: Nationalism and the Technics of Translation in the Spanish Philippines* (Durham, NC: Duke University Press, 2005).

47. Call center enclaves are often given technological sounding names like IT Park in Cebu or Eastwood City Cyberpark in eastern metro Manila.

48. Dan, interview by author, Cebu, July 2012.

49. At the 2019 Metro Manila Film Festival, *Sunod*, to follow in Tagalog, transforms an urban legend among call center agents into a horror movie. In the middle of the graveyard shift, a call center agent hears a child's voice on the other end of the line. The reception is staticky and unclear but the child seems to be crying, then a sudden shriek. The agent espies the shadowy outlines of a child in the dark corridors of the center, once an old hospital witness to many deaths. The child's spirit then follows her home. Movies set in call centers have often been romantic comedies where meet-cute heterosexual romances flourish. Indeed, the call center agent has become a mainstay in urban populations as well as in popular culture over the last two decades. The unusual call center movie allows a slow burn of creepiness that reflects anxieties around night work, ghosts, the undead, possession, abandoned family members, and disembodied voices.

50. JoMar, interview by author, Cebu, July 2012.

51. Marjun Baguio, "According to Study Call Center Agents Prone to HIV-AIDS," *PhilStar*, January 30, 2010. See Padios, *A Nation on Line*.

52. Dan, interview by author, Cebu, July 2012.

53. Gonzalez and Campomanes, "Filipino American Literature," 102.

54. Gonzalez and Campomanes, "Filipino American Literature," 102.

55. Mankekar, *Unsettling India*, 224.

56. Gilles Deleuze, "Postscript on the Societies of Control," *October* 59 (Winter 1992): 6.

57. Deleuze, "Postscript on the Societies of Control," 6.

4 / "We Have No Time to Wallow": Death and Other Timely Diversions

1. Again, I use communality here rather than "community" (or even "friendship," "camaraderie," or "relationship") to underscore the variability in depth, breadth, continuity, coherence, permanence, or ephemerality of the encounters.

2. *Paper Dolls* (*Bubot Niyar*), dir. Tomer Heymann, 2006.

3. Throughout the chapter, I use the characters' names with feminine and masculine pronouns, depending on the situation. I note the contested terrain of gendered terms because of legal and religious constraints and linguistic nonequivalence. Legally in Israel, male caregivers, regardless of gender expression, are hired to take care of male elderly, following Orthodox Jewish practices of modesty. Linguistically, Tagalog, like some other Malayo-Polynesian languages,

does not use gendered pronouns. Also, for a discussion of the cultural and linguistic specificity and capaciousness of *bakla* as a Tagalog term, see Martin Manalansan IV, *Global Divas: Filipino Gay Men in the Diaspora* (Durham, NC: Duke University Press, 2003), 24–25.

4. Maribel Legarda, interview by author, Manila, Philippines, July 2011.

5. Legarda, interview by author, Manila, Philippines, July 2011.

6. *Oxford English Dictionary*, 2nd ed. (Oxford: Oxford University Press, 2004), s.v. "Wallow."

7. As recently as February 2020, Philippine military called upon "national heroes" who might be fooled into funding progressive NGO organizations, like Migrante among others, serving as fronts for the CPP to support the campaign to get rid of local communist armed conflict and infiltration. "Pinoys Abroad Best Asset in Moving PH Forward, AFP Exec Says," *Philippine News Agency*, February 6, 2020.

8. See Claudia Lieblelt's work on Filipino migrants' interpretation of their place in the Holy Land as part of a spiritual and not just economic journey. Claudia Liebelt, "On Global Happenings in the Name of Jesus, Rubbing Shoulders with 'VIPs' and Domestic Work in the 'Holy Land': Notes on Celebrity and Blessing in the Filipino Diaspora," *South East Asia Research* 19, no. 2 (2011): 225–48; and Claudia Liebelt, "'We Are the Jews of Today': Filipino Domestic Workers in Israel and the Language of Diaspora," *Hagar: Studies in Culture, Polity, and Identities* 8, no. 1 (2008): 63–81.

9. Martin F. Manalansan IV, "Queering the Chain of Care Paradigm," *S & F Online* 6, no. 3 (Summer 2008).

10. Patrick Flores, "Palabas," *Ctrl+P Journal of Contemporary Art* 11 (March 2008): 8–99.

11. Doreen Fernandez, *Palabas: Essays on Philippine Theater History* (Loyola Heights, Quezon City: Ateneo de Manila University Press, 1996).

12. Lucy Mae San Pablo Burns, *Puro Arte: Filipinos on the Stages of Empire* (New York: New York University Press, 2013), 144.

13. Ruth Margalit, "Israel's Invisible Filipino Workforce," *New York Times*, May 3, 2017.

14. Ariel Hirschfeld, editorial, *Haaretz* 13 (June 2008): 19.

15. Hirschfeld, editorial.

16. The fact of being old is not what cleaves the speaker from society; indeed in Israel, the elderly are regarded as the repository of memory and as founders/pioneers of the state of Israel. I thank my colleague Leslie Fishbein for this insight. In the movie *Alila* (2003), the Filipino caregiver remains witness and audience to the suffering of a Holocaust survivor with Alzheimer's.

17. The fictional speaker describes Filipinos as "good souls." In my research visit to Israel to speak with residents and Filipino migrants, this is not uncommon "praise" around Israel; they are often described as "*Tuvim anishim*" ("Good people").

18. Liebelt, "'We Are the Jews of Today.'"

19. Rebecca Stein, *Itineraries in Conflict: Israelis, Palestinians, and the Political Lives of Tourism* (Durham, NC: Duke University Press, 2008).

20. In this time period, caregivers could extend another five years under the same employer. In the case of the death of their employer, they are allowed to stay to sit *shiva*. Einat Albin, a lawyer at Tel Aviv University Law Clinic, noted that "*when an*

employer dies, or the contract is discharged for any reason, the migrant worker in practice becomes illegal"—although she explained that, between May 2001 and July 2002, new regulations were introduced allowing a worker in such a position thirty days to find a new employer. Michael Ellman and Smain Laacher, "Migrant Workers in Israel: A Contemporary Form of Slavery," Euro-Mediterranean Human Rights Network and International Federation for Human Rights, 2003.

21. I thank Mary Hawkesworth and Ethel Brooks for this insight.

22. Benedict Anderson, *Imagined Communities: Reflections on the Origin and Spread of Nationalism* (London: Verso, 1987).

23. In Tagalog, personal pronouns are not gender inflected, but in Hebrew and English they are. When speaking Hebrew, Sally often uses the feminine pronoun to refer to herself. In this chapter, I will use the feminine pronoun in English for Sally and sometimes the masculine pronoun for the others.

24. The Ulpan method for Hebrew acquisition for those making *aliyah* is a source of pride for the ministry, given its efficacy for language acquisition.

25. David Eng, *The Feeling of Kinship: Queer Liberalism and the Racialization of Intimacy* (Durham, NC: Duke University Press, 2010), 10–13.

26. *Care Divas*, written by Lisa Magototo, dir. Maribel Legarda, Philippine Educational Theater Association (PETA). Translations mine throughout.

27. Bliss Cua Lim, *Translating Time: Cinema, the Fantastic, and Temporal Critique* (Durham, NC: Duke University Press, 2009), 39.

28. Frederick Engels, *The Origin of the Family, Private Property, and the State* (New York: International Publishers, 1942), 51.

29. See Leopoldina Fortunati, *The Arcane of Reproduction: Housework, Prostitution, Labor and Capital*, trans. Hilary Creek, ed. Jim Fleming. Brooklyn, NY: Autonomedia, 1995.

30. J. Halberstam, *In a Queer Time and Place: Transgender Bodies, Subcultural Lives* (New York: New York University Press, 2005), 2.

31. Sara Ahmed, *The Cultural Politics of Emotion* (Edinburgh: Edinburgh University Press, 2004), 44.

32. See Jasbir Puar, *Terrorist Assemblages: Homonationalism in Queer Times* (Durham, NC: Duke University Press, 2007); and Sunaina Maira, *Jil Oslo: Palestinian Hip Hop, Youth Culture, and the Youth Movement* (Washington, DC: Tadween, 2013).

33. Burns, *Puro Arte*, 142–43.

34. Judith Butler, "Performativity, Precarity, and Sexual Politics," *AIBR, Revista de Antropologia Iberoamericana* 4, no. 3 (2009): vi.

35. Manalansan, "Queering the Chain of Care Paradigm."

36. Manalansan, *Global Divas*.

37. Fenella Cannell, *Power and Intimacy in the Christian Philippines* (Cambridge: Cambridge University Press, 1999), 223.

38. Cannell, *Power and Intimacy in the Christian Philippines*, 213.

39. Catherine Ceniza Choy, *Empire of Care: Nursing and Migration in Filipino American History* (Durham, NC: Duke University Press, 2003).

40. "Chiqui," interview by author, London, 2010, conducted in Tagalog/English/Hebrew. Translation mine.

41. "Victor" (one of the original Paper Dolls), interview by author, Tel Aviv, June 2008.

42. Burns, *Puro Arte*; Theodore S. Gonzalves, *The Day the Dancers Stayed: Performing in the Filipino/American Diaspora* (Philadelphia: Temple University Press, 2010), 19.

Coda: Presence and Mourning to the Future

1. Michael Waters, "The Surprising Intimacy of the Live-Streamed Funeral," *New York Times*, April 2, 2020.

2. Dugan Arnet, "When the Memorial Is Held on Zoom," *Boston Globe*, April 6, 2020.

3. Megan Cerullo, "Funeral Homes Now Livestreaming Memorial Services," CBS News, August 15, 2019.

4. While invoking "face," interface does not quite get at people conjoining but at systems doing so. Coined in the 1960s, the word does suggest connection through boundaries and the boundedness of independent systems.

5. For more on intimacies mediated by technologies, see Valerie Francisco, *The Labor of Care: Filipina Migrants and Transnational Families in the Digital Age* (Urbana: University of Illinois Press, 2018); and Valerie Francisco, "'The Internet Is Magic': Technology, Intimacy, and Transnational Families," *Critical Sociology* 41 (2015): 173–90; also Karen Tongson, *Relocation: Queer Suburban Imaginaries* (New York: New York University Press, 2011).

6. Muslim Filipinos and indigenous peoples in the Philippines from the different island regions have other funerary and mourning rites that do not necessarily include viewing.

7. St. Peter Chapels Website, http://www.stpeter.com.ph.

8. As of 2015, every day six thousand Filipinos leave as contracted OFWs. This does not count those who emigrate to other countries or leave as tourists and stay without authorization.

9. Mortus Magazine, "e-Burol and e-Libing: A Cyberworld Revolution," March 20, 2012, http://mortusmagazine.wordpress.com.

10. For a discussion of the unrepresentable face in Levinas, see Judith Butler, *Precarious Life: The Power of Mourning and Violence* (London: Verso, 2006); see also Charles Veric, "Techniques of the Face: An Essay on Everyday Embodiment, Representation, and Consciousness," PhD diss., Yale University, 2011.

11. Butler, *Precarious Life*, 28.

12. For others, the nature of their work, like domestic and other service work, might not have this easy access to technology during work time.

13. For a discussion of Deleuze's rereading of Foucault's panopticon, see Rey Chow's chapter "Postcolonial Visibilities: Questions Inspired by Deleuze's Method," where she clarifies how through Deleuze Foucault's Eurocentrism might actually be useful to postcolonial framings: Rey Chow, *Entanglements, or Transmedial Thinking about Capture* (Chapel Hill, NC: Duke University Press, 2012).

14. Brian Massumi, *99 Theses on the Revaluation of Value: A Postcapitalist Manifesto* (Minneapolis: University of Minnesota Press, 2018), 68.

15. Pheng Cheah, *What Is a World? On Postcolonial Literature as World Literature* (Durham, NC: Duke University Press, 2016).

16. Cheah, *What Is a World?*, 196.

17. Cheah, *What Is a World?*, 204. Dissatisfied with globalization or cultural difference as the final determinant of imaginings and subject formation, Cheah first

challenges Chakrabarty for his reference to cultural difference as resistant to capital capture: "This view of subalternity's exteriority to capital, however, is perilously close to nostalgia for a pure past that could moreover be a cultural relativist and utopian disavowal of the pervasive reality of capitalist modernization at the socioeconomic level" (204). He then offers Canclini's vision that refuses the opposition between global and local or refusing homogenization or cultural resistance.

18. Cheah, *What Is a World?*, 18.

19. Cheah, *What Is a World?*, 192.

Works cited

ABS-CBN News. "BPOs to Feel Artificial Intelligence 'Reality' in Next 3 to 5 Years: Pernia." *ABS-CBN News*, January 24, 2018.

Ahmed, Sara. *The Cultural Politics of Emotion*. Edinburgh: Edinburgh University Press, 2004.

———. "Orientations: Toward a Queer Phenomenology." *GLQ: Journal of Lesbian and Gay Studies* 12, no. 4 (January 2006): 543–74.

———. *Queer Phenomenology: Orientations, Objects, Others*. Durham, NC: Duke University Press, 2006.

Alvar, Mia. *In the Country*. New York: Knopf, 2015.

Anderson, Benedict. *Imagined Communities: Reflections on the Origin and Spread of Nationalism*. London: Verso, 1987.

———. *Language and Power: Exploring Political Cultures in Indonesia*. Ithaca, NY: Cornell University Press, 1990.

Aquino, Leslie Ann. "40,000 More OFWs Expected to Return Home amid Coronavirus Pandemic." *Manila Bulletin*, May 6, 2020.

Armendral, Aurora. "On Pandemic's Front Lines, Nurses from Half a World Away." *New York Times*, April 20, 2020.

Arnet, Dugan. "When the Memorial Is Held on Zoom." *Boston Globe*, April 6, 2020.

Aviv, Rachel. "The Cost of Caring: The Lives of the Immigrant Women Who Tend to the Needs of Others." *New Yorker*, April 4, 2016.

Baguio, Marjun. "According to Study Call Center Agents Prone to HIV-AIDS." *PhilStar*, January 30, 2010.

Bajaj, Vikas. "A New Capital of Call Centers." *New York Times*, November 25, 2011.

Balance, Christine Bacareza. *Tropical Renditions: Making Musical Scenes in Filipino America*. Durham, NC: Duke University Press, 2016.

Bartlett, Lora. *Migrant Teachers: How American Schools Import Labor.* Cambridge, MA: Harvard University Press, 2014.

Bayot, David Jonathan. "Bienvenido L. Lumbera on Revaluation: The National Stages of Philippine Literature and Its History." *IDEYA: Journal of Humanities* 8, no. 1 (September 2006).

Benedicto, Bobby. *Under Bright Lights: Gay Manila and the Global Scene.* Minneapolis: University of Minnesota Press, 2014.

Benedikt, Amélie Frost. "On Doing the Right Thing at the Right Time." In *Rhetoric and Kairos: Essays in History, Theory, and Praxis,* ed. Phillip Sipiora and James S. Baumlin, 226–35. Albany: State University of New York Press.

Benjamin, Walter. "The Work of Art in the Age of Mechanical Reproduction." In *Illuminations,* trans. Harry Zohn. New York: Schocken, 1969.

Berardi, Franco "Bifo." *The Soul at Work: From Alienation to Autonomy.* Cambridge, MA: MIT Press, 2009.

Bigtas, Jannielyn Ann. "Catriona Gray's Stage Director Shares Training Struggles of the New Miss Universe in Acing the 'Slow-Mo Twirl.'" *GMA News Online,* December 20, 2018.

Bourdieu, Pierre. *The Logic of Practice.* Trans. Richard Nice. Cambridge: Polity, 1990.

Burns, Lucy Mae San Pablo. *Puro Arte: Filipinos on the Stages of Empire.* New York: New York University Press, 2013.

Butler, Judith. "Performativity Precarity and Sexual Politics." *AIBR, Revista de Antropologia Iberoamericana* 4, no. 3 (September–December 2009).

———. *Precarious Life: The Powers of Mourning and Violence.* London: Verso, 2008.

Cannell, Fenella. *Power and Intimacy in the Christian Philippines.* Cambridge: Cambridge University Press, 1999.

Cerullo, Megan. "Funeral Homes Now Livestreaming Memorial Services." *CBS News,* August 15, 2019.

Chakrabarty, Dipesh. *Provincializing Europe: Postcolonial Thought and Historical Difference.* Princeton, NJ: Princeton University Press, 2000.

Cheah, Pheng. *What Is a World? On Postcolonial Literature as World Literature.* Durham, NC: Duke University Press, 2016.

Chow, Rey. *Entanglements, or Transmedial Thinking about Capture.* Durham, NC: Duke University Press, 2012.

Choy, Catherine Ceniza. *Empire of Care: Nursing and Migration in Filipino American History.* Durham, NC: Duke University Press, 2003.

Chuh, Kandice. *The Difference Aesthetics Makes: On the Humanities "After Man."* Durham, NC: Duke University Press, 2019.

Corkery, Michael, and Sapna Maheshwari. "Sympathy Cards Are Selling Out." *New York Times,* April 27, 2020.

Day, Iyko. *Alien Capital: Asian Racialization and the Logic of Settler Colonial Capitalism.* Durham, NC: Duke University Press, 2016.

De Leon, Espie Angelica A. "IBPAP Eyes 1.8-M Jobs in IT-BPM Industry by 2022." *Newsbytes.PH*, April 22, 2018. http://newsbytes.ph/2018/04/22/ibpap -eyes-1-8-m-jobs-in-it-bpm-industry-by-2022.

Deleuze, Gilles. "Postscript on the Societies of Control." *October* 59 (Winter 1992): 3–7.

De Vera, Ben O. "Cash Sent by OFWs Hit Record-High \$2.55B in December— BSP." *Inquirer.net*, February 17, 2017.

———. "OFW Remittances up 5.5% to \$2.3B in May." *Inquirer.Net*, July 18, 2017.

Diaz, Ramona, dir. *The Learning.* CineDiaz Inc., 2011.

Diaz, Robert. "Biyuti from Below: Contemporary Philippine Cinema and the Transing of Kabaklaan." *TSQ* 5, no. 3 (2018): 404–24.

———. "Failed Returns: The Queer Balikbayan in R. Zamora Linmark's *Leche* and Gil Portes's *Miguel Michelle.*" In *Global Asian American Popular Cultures*, ed. Shilpa Davé, Leilani Nishime, and Tasha Oren, 335–50. New York: New York University Press, 2016.

———. "The Limits of *Bakla* and Gay: Feminist Readings of *My Husband's Lover*, Vice Ganda, and Charice Pempengco." *Signs: Journal of Women in Culture and Society* 40, no. 3 (2015): 721–45.

Drew, Rob. *Karaoke Nights: An Ethnographic Rhapsody.* Walnut Creek, CA: Altamira, 2001.

Ellman, Michael, and Smain Laacher. "Migrant Workers in Israel: A Contemporary Form of Slavery." Report from a joint mission to Israel investigating the situation of migrant workers. Copenhagen and Paris: Euro-Mediterranean Human Rights Network and International Federation for Human Rights, 2003.

Eng, David. *The Feeling of Kinship: Queer Liberalism and the Racialization of Intimacy.* Durham, NC: Duke University Press, 2010.

Engels, Frederick. *The Origin of the Family Private Property and the State.* New York: International Publishers, 1942.

Fabros, Alinaya. *Outsourceable Selves: An Ethnography of Call Center Work in a Global Economy of Signs and Selves.* Loyola Heights, Quezon City, Philippines: Ateneo de Manila University Press, 2016.

Fajardo, Kale Bantigue. *Filipino Crosscurrents: Oceanographies of Seafaring, Masculinities, and Globalization.* Minneapolis: University of Minnesota Press, 2011.

Fernandez, Doreen. *Palabas: Essays on Philippine Theater History.* Loyola Heights, Quezon City, Philippines: Ateneo de Manila University Press, 1996.

Flores, Patrick. "Palabas." *Ctrl+P Journal of Contemporary Art* 11 (March 2008): 8–9.

Foucault, Michel. "Of Other Spaces: Utopias and Heterotopias." Trans. Jay Miskowiec. *Diacritics* 16, no. 1 (Spring 1986): 22–27.

Francisco, Valerie. "'The Internet Is Magic': Technology, Intimacy, and Transnational Families." *Critical Sociology* 41, no. 1 (January 2015): 173–90.

——. *The Labor of Care: Filipina Migrants and Transnational Families in the Digital Age.* Urbana: University of Illinois Press, 2018.

Freeman, Elizabeth. *Beside You in Time: Sense-Methods and Queer Sociabilities in Nineteenth-Century America.* Durham, NC: Duke University Press, 2019.

Garcia, J. Neil. *Philippine Gay Culture: The Last Thirty Years: Binabae to Bakla, Silahis to MSM.* Diliman, Quezon City: University of the Philippines Press, 1996.

Glenn, Evelyn Nakano. *Forced to Care: Coercion and Caregiving in America.* Cambridge, MA: Harvard University Press, 2012.

Go, Nathan. "Blind Oracle of Mactan." *American Short Fiction*, April 2, 2018. https://americanshortfiction.org/2018/04/02/blind-oracle-mactan/.

Goldstein, Dana. "Teacher Pay Is So Low in Some U.S. School Districts That They're Recruiting Overseas." *New York Times*, May 3, 2018.

Gonzalez, N. V. M., and Oscar V. Campomanes. "Filipino American Literature." In *An Interethnic Companion to Asian American Literature*, ed. King-Kok Cheung. Cambridge: Cambridge University Press, 1997.

Gonzalves, Theodore S. *The Day the Dancers Stayed: Performing in the Filipino/American Diaspora.* Philadelphia: Temple University Press, 2010.

Gopinath, Gayatri. *Impossible Desires: Queer Diasporas and South Asian Public Cultures.* Durham, NC: Duke University Press, 2005.

——. *Unruly Visions: The Aesthetic Practice of Queer Diaspora.* Durham, NC: Duke University Press, 2018.

Granada, Pio. "BPOs: The Rise of the New Middle Class." *After Call* 5, no. 2 (Midsummer 2012): 10–12.

——. "Last Minute Summer: Four Fantastic Quick Weekend Getaways." *After Call* 5, no. 2 (Midsummer 2012): 16.

Guevarra, Ana Romina. *Marketing Dreams, Manufacturing Heroes: The Transnational Labor Brokering of Filipino Workers.* New Brunswick, NJ: Rutgers University Press, 2009.

Guha, Ranajit. "The Migrant's Time." *Postcolonial Studies: Culture, Politics, Economy* 1, no. 2 (1998): 155–60.

Halberstam, Judith. *In a Queer Time and Place: Transgender Bodies, Subcultural Lives.* New York: New York University Press, 2005.

Hardt, Michael. "Affective Labor." *boundary 2* 26, no. 2 (Summer 1999): 89–100.

Hardt, Michael, and Antonio Negri. *Empire.* Cambridge, MA: Harvard University Press, 2001.

Harney, Stefano, and Fred Moten. *The Undercommons: Fugitive Planning and Black Study.* Wivenhoe: Minor Compositions, 2013.

Harvey, David. *Limits to Capital.* London: Verso, 1982.

Heymann, Tomer, dir. *Paper Dolls (Bubot Niyar).* Claudius Films, L. M. Media, Heymann Brothers Films, the Film Sales Company, 2006.

Hiepko, Andrea Schwwieger. "Europe and the Antilles: An Interview with Édouard Glissant." In *The Creolization of Theory*, ed. Françoise Lionnet and

Shu-mei Shih, trans. Julin Everett, 255–261. Durham, NC: Duke University Press, 2011.

Hirschfeld, Ariel. Editorial. *Haaretz* 13 (June 2008): 19.

Hochschild, Arlie. *The Managed Heart: Commercialization of Human Feeling*. Berkeley: University of California Press, 1983.

Hong, Grace Kyungwon. "Speculative Surplus: Asian American Racialization and the Neoliberal Shift." *Social Text* 36, no. 2 (June 2018): 107–22.

Kincaid, Jamaica. *A Small Place*. New York: Farrar, Straus, Giroux, 1988.

Kristeva, Julia. *Powers of Horror: An Essay on Abjection*. New York: Columbia University Press, 1982.

Legarda, Maribel, dir. *Care Divas*. Written by Lisa Magtoto, music and lyrics by Vincent De Jesus. Philippine Educational Theater Association (PETA). Manila, Philippines, July 2011–July 2017.

Lerma, Karen. "Rise of Machines: Philippines Outsourcing Industry Braces for AI." *Reuters*, November 8, 2017.

Liebelt, Claudia. "On Global Happenings in the Name of Jesus, Rubbing Shoulders with 'VIPs' and Domestic Work in the 'Holy Land': Notes on Celebrity and Blessing in the Filipino Diaspora." *South East Asia Research* 19, no. 2 (June 2011): 225–48.

———. "'We Are the Jews of Today:' Filipino Domestic Workers in Israel and the Language of Diaspora." *Hagar: Studies in Culture, Polity, and Identities* 8, no. 1 (January 2008): 63–81.

Lim, Bliss Cua. *Translating Time: Cinema, the Fantastic, and Temporal Critique*. Durham, NC: Duke University Press, 2009.

Lowe, Lisa. *The Intimacies of Four Continents*. Durham, N: Duke University Press, 2015.

Lumbera, Bienvenido. "'Dating': Panimulang Muni sa Estetika ng Panitikang Filipino." *Lagda* 1 (1999).

Magtulis, Prinz. "As 'Few' Firms Seek Cash Aid, BPOs Still Seen as 'One of Big Winners' of Pandemic." *PhilStar*, April 30, 2020.

Maira, Sunaina. *Jil Oslo: Palestinian Hip Hop, Youth Culture, and the Youth Movement*. Washington, DC: Tadween, 2013.

Manalansan IV, Martin. *Global Divas: Filipino Gay Men in the Diaspora*. Durham, NC: Duke University Press, 2003.

———. "Messy Mismeasure: Exploring the Wilderness of Queer Migrant Lives." *South Atlantic Quarterly* 11, no. 3 (July 2018): 491–506.

———. "Queer Intersections: Sexuality and Gender in Migration Studies." *International Migration Review* 40, no. 1 (Spring 2006): 224–49.

———. "Queering the Chain of Care Paradigm." *S & F Online* 6, no. 3 (Summer 2008).

———. "Servicing the World: Flexible Filipinos and the Unsecured Life." In *Political Emotions: New Agendas in Communication*, ed. Janet Staiger, Ann Cvetkovich, and Ann Reynolds, 215–28. London: Routledge, 2010.

———. "Wayward Erotics: Mediating Queer Diasporic Return." In *Media, Erotics, and Transnational Asia*, ed. Purnima Mankekar and Louisa Schein, 33–51. Durham, NC: Duke University Press, 2012.

Mankekar, Purnima. *Unsettling India: Affect, Temporality, Transnationality.* Durham, NC: Duke University Press, 2015.

Margalit, Ruth. "Israel's Invisible Filipino Workforce." *New York Times*, May 3, 2017.

Marte-Wood, Alden. "Philippine Reproductive Fiction and Crises of Social Reproduction." *Post 45*, issue 1: "Deindustrialization and the New Cultures of Work" (2019).

Marx, Karl. *Capital.* Vol. 1. Trans. Ben Fowkes. London: Penguin, 1976.

Massumi, Brian. *99 Theses on the Revaluation of Value: A Postcapitalist Manifesto.* Minneapolis: University of Minnesota Press, 2018.

———. *Parables for the Virtual: Movement, Affect, Sensation.* Durham, NC: Duke University Press, 2002.

Mathur, Saloni. *The Migrant's Time: Rethinking Art History and Diaspora.* Williamstown, MA: Sterling and Francine Clark Art Institute, 2011.

McFarling, Usha Lee. "Coronavirus Taking Outsized Toll on Filipino American Nurses." *STATNews*, April 28, 2020.

Mortus. "e-Burol and e-Libing: A Cyberworld Revolution." March 20, 2012. http://mortusmagazine.wordpress.com/2012/03/20/e-burol-and-e-libing-a -cyberworld-revolution.

Munawwar, Mihammad. *Ocean States: Archipelagic Regimes in the Law of the Sea.* Dordrecht: Martinus Nijhoff, 1995.

Muñoz, Jose Esteban. *Cruising Utopia: The Then and There of Queer Futurity.* New York: New York University Press, 2009.

Nichols, Bill. *Introduction to Documentary.* 2nd ed. Bloomington: Indiana University Press, 2010.

Padios, Jan. "Listening between the Lines: Culture, Difference, and Immaterial Labor in the Philippine Call Center Industry." PhD diss., New York University, 2012.

———. *A Nation on the Line: Call Centers as Postcolonial Predicaments in the Philippines.* Durham, NC: Duke University Press, 2018.

———. "Queer Confessions: Transgression, Affect, and National Crisis in the Philippines' Call Center Industry." *Center for Art + Thought.* http:// centerforartandthought.org.

Parreñas, Rhacel. *Servants of Globalization: Migration and Domestic Work.* Stanford, CA: Stanford University Press, 2001.

Patel, Reena. *Working the Night Shift: Women in India's Call Center Industry.* Stanford, CA: Stanford University Press, 2010.

Philippine News Agency. "Pinoys Abroad Best Asset in Moving PH Forward, AFP Exec Says." February 6, 2020.

Pratt, Mary Louise. "The Short Story: The Long and the Short of It." *Poetics* 10 (1981): 175–94.

Puar, Jasbir. *Terrorist Assemblages: Homonationalism in Queer Times.* Durham, NC: Duke University Press, 2007.

Puri, Shalini. "Finding the Field: Notes on Caribbean Cultural Criticism, Area Studies, and the Forms of Engagement." *Small Axe* 41, no. 2 (July 2013): 58–73.

Rafael, Vicente. *The Promise of the Foreign: Nationalism and the Technics of Translation in the Spanish Philippines.* Durham, NC: Duke University Press, 2005.

———. "Writing Outside: On the Question of Location," In *Discrepant Histories: Translocal Essays on Filipino Cultures,* ed. Vicente Rafael, xiii–xxviii. Philadelphia: Temple University Press, 1995.

Roberts, Brian Russell, and Michelle Stephens. "Archipelagic American Studies and the Caribbean." *Journal of Transnational American Studies* 5, no. 1 (2013): 1–20.

Rodriguez, Robyn. *Migrants for Export: How the Philippine State Brokers Labor to the World.* Minneapolis: University of Minnesota Press, 2010.

Roediger, David. *The Production of Difference: Race and the Management of Labor in US History.* Oxford: Oxford University Press, 2012.

San Juan, Alexandria. "Almost 17,000 Repatriated OFWs Have Been Tested for COVID-19—DOTR." *Manila Bulletin,* May 13, 2020.

Santa Ana, Jeffrey. *Racial Feelings: Asian America in a Capitalist Culture of Emotion.* Philadelphia: Temple University Press, 2015.

Sedgwick, Eve Kosofsky. "Queer Performativity: Henry James's Art of the Novel." *GLQ: Journal of Lesbian and Gay Studies* 1, no. 1 (1993): 1–16.

———. *Touching Feeling: Affect, Pedagogy, Performance.* Durham, NC: Duke University Press, 2003.

See, Sarita Echavez. *The Filipino Primitive: Accumulation and Resistance in the American Museum.* New York: New York University Press, 2017.

Shome, Raka. "Thinking through the Diaspora: Call Centers, India, and a New Politics of Hybridity." *International Journal of Cultural Studies* 9, no. 1 (March 2006): 105–24.

Skinner, Michelle Cruz. *In the Company of Strangers.* Honolulu, HI: Bamboo Ridge.

Spivak, Gayatri Chakravorty. "Can the Subaltern Speak?" In *Marxism and the Interpretation of Culture,* ed. Cary Nelson and Lawrence Grossberg, 271–313. Urbana: University of Illinois Press, 1988.

Stein, Rebecca. *Itineraries in Conflict: Israelis, Palestinians, and the Political Lives of Tourism.* Durham, NC: Duke University Press, 2008.

Stewart, Kathleen. *Ordinary Affects.* Durham, NC: Duke University Press, 2007.

Tadiar, Neferti. "Decolonization, 'Race,' and Remaindered Life under Empire." In *Critical Ethnic Studies: A Reader,* ed. Nada Elia et al., 395–415. Durham, NC: Duke University Press, 2016.

———. *Fantasy-Production: Sexual Economies and Other Philippine Consequences for the New World Order.* Manila: Ateneo de Manila University Press, 2004.

———. "Life-Times in Fate Playing." *South Atlantic Quarterly* 111, no. 4 (Fall 2012): 783–802.

———. "Life-Times of Becoming Human." *Occasion: Interdisciplinary Studies in the Humanities* 3 (March 2012).

———. "Life-Times of Disposability within Global Neoliberalism." *Social Text* 31, no. 2 (Summer 2013): 19–48.

Thompson, Roger. "Ralph Waldo Emerson and the American *Kairos*." In *Rhetoric and Kairos: Essays in History, Theory, and Praxis*, ed. Phillip Sipiora and James S. Baumlin, 187–98. Albany: State University of New York Press.

Tillich, Paul. *The Eternal Now.* New York: Charles Scribner's Sons, 1963.

Tomba, Massimiliano. *Marx's Temporalities.* Leiden: Brill, 2012.

Tongson, Karen. *Relocation: Queer Suburban Imaginaries.* New York: New York University Press, 2011.

Tsing, Anna. *Friction: An Ethnography of Global Connection.* Princeton, NJ: Princeton University Press, 2005.

Vargas, Jose Antonio. *Dear America: Notes of an Undocumented Citizen.* New York: Dey Street, 2018.

———, dir. *Documented.* CNN Films and Apo Anak Productions, 2013.

Vergara, Benito. *Pinoy Capital: The Filipino Nation in Daly City.* Philadelphia: Temple University Press, 2009.

Veric, Charlie Samuya. "Techniques of the Face: An Essay on Everyday Embodiment, Representation, and Consciousness." PhD diss., Yale University 2011.

Virno, Paolo. "The Ambivalence of Disenchantment." In *Radical Thought in Italy: A Potential Politics*, ed. Paolo Virno and Michael Hardt. Minneapolis: University of Minnesota Press, 1996.

Vora, Kalindi. *Life Support: Biocapital and the New History of Outsourced Labor.* Minneapolis: University of Minnesota Press, 2015.

Waters, Michael. "The Surprising Intimacy of the Live-Streamed Funeral." *New York Times*, April 2, 2020.

Weeks, Kathi. *The Problem with Work: Feminism, Marxism, Antiwork Politics, and Postwork Imaginaries.* Durham, NC: Duke University Press, 2011.

Index

call center industry (*continued*)
74; revenue, 68; scholarly work on, 69–70, 76; three-hundred-second rule, 68, 69, 72, 79, 81; work time in, 18
call center workers: background and education of, 68, 84, 85–86; bodily representation of, 85; daily life of, 87, 90; dispersed nationality of, 88; emotions of, 81; empathy of, 79–81; English-language proficiency of, 76, 77; futures of, 84, 89; immaterial labor of, 139n3; interpersonal skills of, 77–78; interviews with, 70, 76–77; living conditions of, 76; as mediators, 71–73; night shifts, 76, 87–88; offshoreness of, 19, 71–72, 73, 75; promotional image of, 71–73, 72, 73, 75, 89–90, 140n12; public perception of, 86–87, 88; quality control of, 80; recruitment of, 68, 77, 82, 83–84, 85–86; repetitive work of, 81, 82, 85; survivalist tactics of, 84; temporal migration of, 88–89; training of, 78–79, 80–81; wages, 77, 83, 85
Campomanes, Oscar, 47, 75, 89
Canclini, Néstor García, 145n17
Cannell, Fenella, 27, 112, 113
Care Divas (musical): affective diversions in, 20, 94; bodily transformation in, 110–11; critique of nation-state, 106, 111–12; death motif, 20, 92, 94, 96, 108–10; depiction of love, 106, 109–10; emotional turns, 95–96, 98; familial responsibilities in, 103–6; feeling of stuckness, 104; finale, 92, 97, 114; hero/victim binary, 20; lyrics of, 114; Middle East conflict in, 107; minor characters, 94; opening scene, 91–92, 94; plotline of, 92, 94–95, 96, 114; refusal to wallow, 95, 96, 97, 98; scenes from, 93; shows, 94, 95, 112; source material, 94; two worlds of, 110–11; unsanctioned relationships in, 106–7, 108
care labor: creativity of, 12; cultural aspects of, 12, 18; gender and, 12, 15; human touch of, 20–21; of love, 10; proximity and propinquity of, 11–12; relations of action and feeling in, 10–11; trans-subjectivity of, 15
Chakrabarty, Dipesh, 145n17
Charlene (Charlene Marilynn Oliver): "I've Never Been to Me," 34, 136n17
chattel slavery, 132n14
Cheah, Pheng, 124, 125, 144n17
Chow, Rey, 2, 7

chronic in-between, 43, 44
chronics, 132n11
chronography, 19, 20, 67, 69, 89
Chuh, Kandice, 136n11; *The Difference Aesthetic Makes*, 26
class promiscuity, 86
collective present, 7
colonial relations, 133nn24,27, 134n29
communality, 6, 16, 20, 21
contract labor, 12–13, 137n21
cooperation networks, 15
creative labor, 14
currency conversion, 48

dating (arrival): aesthetics of, 26; as affect, 27; centrifugal, 26; communal nature of, 27; definition of, 18–19, 24, 25, 36, 42, 136n9; as disruptive event, 39–40; effect on time and place, 27, 42; as embodied journey, 27–28, 32–33; as form of nonverbal address, 27; gender and, 26; as possibility, 40; as refusing redemption, 34; as unproductive world-making, 40
Day, Iyko, 134n32; *Alien Labor*, 14
death motif, 18, 20, 64, 92, 94, 96, 108–10
debt of obligation, 31, 65–66, 123
decolonization: temporality of, 125
Deleuze, Gilles, 67, 68, 89
Diaz, Ramona, 23–24, 26. See also *The Learning* (film)
digital connectivity, 7
digital mourning, 116, 117
directionality, 10, 133n19; and diversion, 39, 81, 94, 98, 114
disaffection, 96–97
disciplinary society, 89
displacement, 37
domestic workers: abusive behavior of, 55, 61–62; commodified labor of, 61; death of, 62; exploitation of, 132n14; in geriatric care, 99; household rhythm and, 52; identities of, 56, 57; in-between time, 47–48; invisibility of, 55, 57, 98–99, 111; in Israel, 98–99, 141n3, 142nn16,20; in Italy, 45, 46; legal status of, 46, 142n20; lives in apposition, 53–54; as miracle workers, 56; opportunistic frenzy of, 46–47; as performers, 102–3; personal relationships of, 48, 49–50; relationship with place, 51, 52; resistance of, 59, 61; sense of continuity, 51–52; social status of, 56–57; suicides of, 55; work cycle of, 50–51; xenophobia toward, 107–8

ALLAN PUNZALAN ISAAC is Professor of American Studies and English at Rutgers University, New Brunswick, NJ. His book *American Tropics: Articulating Filipino America* (Minnesota, 2006) is the recipient of the Association for Asian American Studies Cultural Studies Book Award.

www.ingramcontent.com/pod-product-compliance
Lightning Source LLC
Chambersburg PA
CBHW032145020426
42334CB00016B/1225